Visit Cram101.com for full Practice Exams

Visit Cram101.com for full Practice Exams

Textbook Outlines, Highlights, and Practice Quizzes

Friedland and Relyea Environmental Science for AP

by Andrew Friedland, 1st Edition

All "Just the Facts101" Material Written or Prepared by Cram101 Publishing

Title Page

Visit Cram101.com for full Practice Exams

WHY STOP HERE... THERE'S MORE ONLINE

With technology and experience, we've developed tools that make studying easier and efficient. Like this Cram101 textbook notebook, **Cram101.com** offers you the highlights from every chapter of your actual textbook. However, unlike this notebook, **Cram101.com** gives you practice tests for each of the chapters. You also get access to in-depth reference material for writing essays and papers.

By purchasing this book, you get 50% off the normal subscription free!. Just enter the promotional code **'DK73DW23086'** on the Cram101.com registration screen.

CRAM101.COM FEATURES:

Outlines & Highlights
Just like the ones in this notebook, but with links to additional information.

Integrated Note Taking
Add your class notes to the Cram101 notes, print them and maximize your study time.

Problem Solving
Step-by-step walk throughs for math, stats and other disciplines.

Practice Exams
Five different test taking formats for every chapter.

Easy Access
Study any of your books, on any computer, anywhere.

Unlimited Textbooks
All the features above for virtually all your textbooks, just add them to your account at no additional cost.

Be sure to use the promo code above when registering on Cram101.com to get 50% off your membership fees.

Visit Cram101.com for full Practice Exams

STUDYING MADE EASY

This Cram101 notebook is designed to make studying easier and increase your comprehension of the textbook material. Instead of starting with a blank notebook and trying to write down everything discussed in class lectures, you can use this Cram101 textbook notebook and annotate your notes along with the lecture.

Our goal is to give you the best tools for success.

For a supreme understanding of the course, pair your notebook with our online tools. Should you decide you prefer Cram101.com as your study tool,

we'd like to offer you a trade...

Our Trade In program is a simple way for us to keep our promise and provide you the best studying tools, regardless of where you purchased your Cram101 textbook notebook. As long as your notebook is in *Like New Condition**, you can send it back to us and we will immediately give you a Cram101.com account free for 120 days!

Let The Trade In Begin!

THREE SIMPLE STEPS TO TRADE:

1. Go to www.cram101.com/tradein and fill out the packing slip information.

2. Submit and print the packing slip and mail it in with your Cram101 textbook notebook.

3. Activate your account after you receive your email confirmation.

* Books must be returned in *Like New Condition*, meaning there is no damage to the book including, but not limited to; ripped or torn pages, markings or writing on pages, or folded / creased pages. Upon receiving the book, Cram101 will inspect it and reserves the right to terminate your free Cram101.com account and return your textbook notebook at the owners expense.

Visit Cram101.com for full Practice Exams

"Just the Facts101" is a Cram101 publication and tool designed to give you all the facts from your textbooks. Visit Cram101.com for the full practice test for each of your chapters for virtually any of your textbooks.

Cram101 has built custom study tools specific to your textbook. We provide all of the factual testable information and unlike traditional study guides, we will never send you back to your textbook for more information.

YOU WILL NEVER HAVE TO HIGHLIGHT A BOOK AGAIN!

Cram101 StudyGuides
All of the information in this StudyGuide is written specifically for your textbook. We include the key terms, places, people, and concepts... the information you can expect on your next exam!

Want to take a practice test?
Throughout each chapter of this StudyGuide you will find links to cram101.com where you can select specific chapters to take a complete test on, or you can subscribe and get practice tests for up to 12 of your textbooks, along with other exclusive cram101.com tools like problem solving labs and reference libraries.

Cram101.com
Only cram101.com gives you the outlines, highlights, and PRACTICE TESTS specific to your textbook. Cram101.com is an online application where you'll discover study tools designed to make the most of your limited study time.

By purchasing this book, you get 50% off the normal monthly subscription fee!. Just enter the promotional code **'DK73DW23086'** on the Cram101.com registration screen.

www.Cram101.com

Copyright © 2013 by Cram101, Inc. All rights reserved.
"Just the FACTS101"®, "Cram101"® and "Never Highlight a Book Again!"® are registered trademarks of Cram101, Inc.
ISBN(s): 9781490244686. PUBE-4.2013914

Visit Cram101.com for full Practice Exams

facts101

Friedland and Relyea Environmental Science for AP
Andrew Friedland, 1st

CONTENTS

1. Studying the State of Our Earth 5
2. Environmental Systems 13
3. Ecosystem Ecology 25
4. Global Climates and Biomes 35
5. Evolution of Biodiversity 47
6. Population and Community Ecology 55
7. The Human Population 63
8. Earth Systems 69
9. Water Resources 81
10. Land, Public and Private 89
11. Feeding the World 97
12. Nonrenewable Energy Sources 107
13. Achieving Energy Sustainability 114
14. Water Pollution 121
15. Air Pollution and Stratospheric Ozone Depletion 129
16. Waste Generation and Waste Disposal 135
17. Human Health and Environmental Risks 142
18. Conservation of Biodiversity 150
19. Global Change 158
20. Sustainability, Economics, and Equity 166

Visit Cram101.com for full Practice Exams

1. Studying the State of Our Earth

CHAPTER OUTLINE: KEY TERMS, PEOPLE, PLACES, CONCEPTS

Abiotic component

Biotic component

Ecosystem

Environment

Environmental science

First law of thermodynamics

Biodiversity

Ecosystem services

Environmental indicator

Species diversity

Conservation

Tiger

Greenhouse effect

Resource depletion

Development

Sustainable development

Ecological footprint

Deductive reasoning

Inductive reasoning

Replication

Chlorpyrifos

Visit Cram101.com for full Practice Exams

1. Studying the State of Our Earth
CHAPTER OUTLINE: KEY TERMS, PEOPLE, PLACES, CONCEPTS

Critical thinking

Environmental justice

CHAPTER HIGHLIGHTS & NOTES: KEY TERMS, PEOPLE, PLACES, CONCEPTS

Abiotic component	In ecology and biology, abiotic components (also called abiotic factors) are non-living chemical and physical factors in the environment, which affect ecosystems. Abiotic phenomena underlie all of biology. In biology, abiotic factors can be classified as light or more generally radiation, temperature, water, atmospheric gases, or soil.
Biotic component	Biotic components are the living things that shape an ecosystem. A biotic factor is any living component that affects another organism, including animals that consume the organism in question, and the living food that the organism consumes. Each biotic factor needs energy to do work and food for proper growth.
Ecosystem	An ecosystem is a community of living organisms (plants, animals and microbes) in conjunction with the nonliving components of their environment (things like air, water and mineral soil), interacting as a system. These components are regarded as linked together through nutrient cycles and energy flows. As ecosystems are defined by the network of interactions among organisms, and between organisms and their environment, they can come in any size but usually encompass specific, limited spaces (although some scientists say that the entire planet is an ecosystem).
Environment	The biophysical environment is the biotic and abiotic surrounding of an organism, or population, and includes particularly the factors that have an influence in their survival, development and evolution. The naked term environment can make reference to different concepts, but it is often used as a short form for the biophysical environment. This practice is common, for instance, among governments, that usually name their departments and agencies dealing with the biophysical environment with denominations like Environment Agency.
Environmental science	Environmental science is a multidisciplinary academic field that integrates physical and biological sciences, (including but not limited to ecology, physics, chemistry, biology, soil science, geology, atmospheric science and geography) to the study of the environment, and the solution of environmental problems. Environmental science provides an integrated, quantitative, and interdisciplinary approach to the study of environmental systems.

Visit Cram101.com for full Practice Exams

1. Studying the State of Our Earth

CHAPTER HIGHLIGHTS & NOTES: KEY TERMS, PEOPLE, PLACES, CONCEPTS

First law of thermodynamics	ImgProperty databaseimg The first law of thermodynamics is a version of the law of conservation of energy, specialized for thermodynamical systems. It is usually formulated by stating that the change in the internal energy of a closed system is equal to the amount of heat supplied to the system, minus the amount of work performed by the system on its surroundings. The law of conservation of energy can be stated: The energy of an isolated system is constant.
Biodiversity	Biodiversity is the degree of variation of life forms within a given species, ecosystem, biome, or an entire planet. Biodiversity is a measure of the health of ecosystems. Biodiversity is in part a function of climate.
Ecosystem services	Humankind benefits from a multitude of resources and processes that are supplied by natural ecosystems. Collectively, these benefits are known as ecosystem services and include products like clean drinking water and processes such as the decomposition of wastes. While scientists and environmentalists have discussed ecosystem services for decades, these services were popularized and their definitions formalized by the United Nations 2004 Millennium Ecosystem Assessment (MA), a four-year study involving more than 1,300 scientists worldwide.
Environmental indicator	Environmental indicators are simple measures that tell us what is happening in the environment. Since the environment is very complex, indicators provide a more practical and economical way to track the state of the environment than if we attempted to record every possible variable in the environment. For example, concentrations of ozone depleting substances (ODS) in the atmosphere, tracked over time, is a good indicator with respect to the environmental issue of stratospheric ozone depletion..
Species diversity	Species diversity is the effective number of different species that are represented in a collection of individuals (a dataset). The effective number of species refers to the number of equally-abundant species needed to obtain the same mean proportional species abundance as that observed in the dataset of interest . Species diversity consists of two components, species richness and species evenness.
Conservation	Conservation is an ethic of resour use, allocation, and protection. Its primary focus is upon maintaining the health of the natural world: its, fisheries, habitats, and biological diversity. Secondary focus is on materials conservation and energy conservation, which are seen as important to protect the natural world.
Tiger	The tiger is the largest cat species, reaching a total body length of up to 3.3 metres (11 ft) and weighing up to 306 kg (670 lb). Their most recognizable feature is a pattern of dark vertical stripes on reddish-orange fur with lighter underparts.

Visit Cram101.com for full Practice Exams

1. Studying the State of Our Earth

CHAPTER HIGHLIGHTS & NOTES: KEY TERMS, PEOPLE, PLACES, CONCEPTS

Greenhouse effect	The greenhouse effect is a process by which thermal radiation from a planetary surface is absorbed by atmospheric greenhouse gases, and is re-radiated in all directions. Since part of this re-radiation is back towards the surface, energy is transferred to the surface and the lower atmosphere. As a result, the avera surface temperature is higher than it would be if direct heating by solar radiation were the only warming mechanism.
Resource depletion	Resource depletion is the exhaustion of raw materials within a region. Resources are commonly divided between renewable resources and non-renewable resources. Use of either of these forms of resources beyond their rate of replacement is considered to be resource depletion.
Development	In classical differential geometry, development refers to the simple idea of rolling one smooth surface over another in Euclidean space. For example, the tangent plane to a surface (such as the sphere or the cylinder) at a point can be rolled around the surface to obtain the tangent-plane at other points. The tangential contact between the surfaces being rolled over one another provides a relation between points on the two surfaces.
Sustainable development	Sustainable development is a pattern of growth in which resource use aims to meet human needs while preserving the environment so that these needs can be met not only in the present, but also for generations to come (sometimes taught as ELF-Environment, Local people, Future). The term sustainable development was used by the Brundtland Commission which coined what has become the most often-quoted definition of sustainable development as development that 'meets the needs of the present without compromising the ability of future generations to meet their own needs.' Sustainable development ties together concern for the carrying capacity of natural systems with the social challenges facing humanity. As early as the 1970s 'sustainability' was employed to describe an economy 'in equilibrium with basic ecological support systems.' Ecologists have pointed to The Limits to Growth, and presented the alternative of a 'steady state economy' in order to address environmental concerns.
Ecological footprint	The ecological footprint is a measure of human demand on the Earth's ecosystems. It is a standardized measure of demand for natural capital that may be contrasted with the planet's ecological capacity to regenerate. It represents the amount of biologically productive land and sea area necessary to supply the resources a human population consumes, and to assimilate associated waste.
Deductive reasoning	Deductive reasoning, is reasoning which constructs or evaluates deductive arguments. Deductive reasoning contrasts with inductive reasoning in that a specific conclusion is arrived at from a general principle. Deductive arguments are attempts to show that a conclusion necessarily follows from a set of premises or hypotheses.

Visit Cram101.com for full Practice Exams

1. Studying the State of Our Earth

CHAPTER HIGHLIGHTS & NOTES: KEY TERMS, PEOPLE, PLACES, CONCEPTS

Inductive reasoning	Inductive reasoning, is a kind of reasoning that constructs or evaluates propositions that are abstractions of observations of individual instances of members of the same class. Inductive reasoning contrasts with deductive reasoning in that a general conclusion is arrived at by specific examples. However, philosophically the definition is much more nuanced than simple progression from particular / individual instances to wider generalizations.
Replication	Replication, in metallography, is the use of thin plastic films to nondestructively duplicate the microstructure of a component. The film is then examined at high magnifications. Replication is a method of copying the topography of a surface by casting or impressing material onto the surface.
Chlorpyrifos	Chlorpyrifos is a crystalline organophosphate insecticide that inhibits acetylcholinesterase and is used to control insect pests. Trade names include Brodan, Detmol UA, Dowco 179, Dursban, Empire, Eradex, Lorsban, Paqeant, Piridane, Scout, and Stipend. Chlorpyrifos is moderately toxic and chronic exposure has been linked to neurological effects, developmental disorders, and autoimmune disorders.
Critical thinking	Critical thinking is the process of thinking that questions assumptions. It is a way of deciding whether a claim is true, false; sometimes true, or partly true. The origins of critical thinking can be traced in Western thought to the Socratic method of Ancient Greece and in the East, to the Buddhist kalama sutta and Abhidharma.
Environmental justice	The term environmental justice emerged as a concept in the United States in the early 1980s. The term has two distinct uses. The first and more common usage describes a social movement in the United States whose focus is on the fair distribution of environmental benefits and burdens.

Visit Cram101.com for full Practice Exams

1. Studying the State of Our Earth

CHAPTER QUIZ: KEY TERMS, PEOPLE, PLACES, CONCEPTS

1. _____ is the degree of variation of life forms within a given species, ecosystem, biome, or an entire planet. _____ is a measure of the health of ecosystems. _____ is in part a function of climate.

   a. Biological monitoring working party
   b. Biometeorology
   c. Bioreporter
   d. Biodiversity

2. _____, is a kind of reasoning that constructs or evaluates propositions that are abstractions of observations of individual instances of members of the same class. _____ contrasts with deductive reasoning in that a general conclusion is arrived at by specific examples. Definition of _____

   However, philosophically the definition is much more nuanced than simple progression from particular / individual instances to wider generalizations.

   a. Argument from analogy
   b. Enumerative induction
   c. Imperfect induction
   d. Inductive reasoning

3. _____, in metallography, is the use of thin plastic films to nondestructively duplicate the microstructure of a component. The film is then examined at high magnifications.

   _____ is a method of copying the topography of a surface by casting or impressing material onto the surface.

   a. Roasting
   b. Scheil equation
   c. Sclerometer
   d. Replication

4. An _____ is a community of living organisms (plants, animals and microbes) in conjunction with the nonliving components of their environment (things like air, water and mineral soil), interacting as a system. These components are regarded as linked together through nutrient cycles and energy flows. As _____s are defined by the network of interactions among organisms, and between organisms and their environment, they can come in any size but usually encompass specific, limited spaces (although some scientists say that the entire planet is an _____).

   a. Odyssey
   b. Ecosystem
   c. Cascade effect
   d. Chreod

5. . The _____ is a process by which thermal radiation from a planetary surface is absorbed by atmospheric greenhouse gases, and is re-radiated in all directions.

Visit Cram101.com for full Practice Exams

1. Studying the State of Our Earth

CHAPTER QUIZ: KEY TERMS, PEOPLE, PLACES, CONCEPTS

Since part of this re-radiation is back towards the surface, energy is transferred to the surface and the lower atmosphere. As a result, the avera surface temperature is higher than it would be if direct heating by solar radiation were the only warming mechanism.

a. Polar amplification
b. Greenhouse effect
c. Runaway greenhouse effect
d. Homogenization

Visit Cram101.com for full Practice Exams

ANSWER KEY
1. Studying the State of Our Earth

1. d

2. d

3. d

4. b

5. b

You can take the complete Chapter Practice Test

for 1. Studying the State of Our Earth
on all key terms, persons, places, and concepts.

Online 99 Cents

http://www.epub89.16.23086.1.cram101.com/

Use www.Cram101.com for all your study needs

including Cram101's online interactive problem solving labs in

chemistry, statistics, mathematics, and more.

Visit Cram101.com for full Practice Exams

2. Environmental Systems

CHAPTER OUTLINE: KEY TERMS, PEOPLE, PLACES, CONCEPTS

Atom

Molecule

Mass number

Radioactive decay

Chemical bond

Hydrogen bond

Ionic bond

Covalent bond

Capillary action

Surface tension

Polar

Chemical reaction

Enzyme

Macromolecule

Organic compound

Polysaccharide

Photon

Kinetic energy

Potential energy

Chemical energy

First law of thermodynamics

Visit Cram101.com for full Practice Exams

2. Environmental Systems
CHAPTER OUTLINE: KEY TERMS, PEOPLE, PLACES, CONCEPTS

Second law of thermodynamics

Energy quality

Energy transformation

Available energy

Conversion

Open system

Systems analysis

Energy flow

Steady state

Negative feedback loop

Sustainable management

Ozone layer

Catalyst

Montreal Protocol

Visit Cram101.com for full Practice Exams

2. Environmental Systems

CHAPTER HIGHLIGHTS & NOTES: KEY TERMS, PEOPLE, PLACES, CONCEPTS

Atom	In the mathematical field of order theory, given two elements a and b of a partially ordered set, one says that b covers a, and writes a <: b or b :> a, if a < b and there is no element c such that a < c < b. In other words, b covers a if b is greater than a and minimal with this property, or equivalently if a is smaller than b and maximal with this property. In a partially ordered set with least element 0, an atom is an element that covers 0, i.e. an element that is minimal among the non-zero elements.
Molecule	A molecule is an electrically neutral group of two or more atoms held together by covalent chemical bonds. Molecules are distinguished from ions by their electrical charge. However, in quantum physics, organic chemistry, and biochemistry, the term molecule is often used less strictly, also being applied to polyatomic ions.
Mass number	The mass number also called atomic mass number, is the total number of protons and neutrons (together known as nucleons) in an atomic nucleus. Because protons and neutrons both are baryons, the mass number A is identical with the baryon number B as of the nucleus as of the whole atom or ion. The mass number is different for each different isotope of a chemical element.
Radioactive decay	Radioactive decay is the process by which an atomic nucleus of an unstable atom loses energy by emitting ionizing particles (ionizing radiation) A decay, or loss of energy, results when an atom with one type of nucleus, called the parent radionuclide, transforms to an atom with a nucleus in a different state, or to a different nucleus containing different numbers of nucleons.
Chemical bond	A chemical bond is an attraction between atoms that allows the formation of chemical substances that contain two or more atoms. The bond is caused by the electromagnetic force attraction between opposite charges, either between electrons and nuclei, or as the result of a dipole attraction. The strength of chemical bonds varies considerably; there are 'strong bonds' such as covalent or ionic bonds and 'weak bonds' such as dipole-dipole interactions, the London dispersion force and hydrogen bonding.
Hydrogen bond	A hydrogen bond is the attractive interaction of a hydrogen atom with an electronegative atom, such as nitrogen, oxygen or fluorine, that comes from another molecule or chemical group. The hydrogen must be covalently bonded to another electronegative atom to create the bond. These bonds can occur between molecules (intermolecularly), or within different parts of a single molecule (intramolecularly).
Ionic bond	An ionic bond is a type of chemical bond formed through an electrostatic attraction between two oppositely charged ions. Ionic bonds are formed between a cation, which is usually a metal, and an anion, which is usually a nonmetal. Pure ionic bonding cannot exist: all ionic compounds have some degree of covalent bonding.

Visit Cram101.com for full Practice Exams

2. Environmental Systems

CHAPTER HIGHLIGHTS & NOTES: KEY TERMS, PEOPLE, PLACES, CONCEPTS

Covalent bond	A covalent bond is a form of chemical bonding that is characterized by the sharing of pairs of electrons between atoms. The stable balance of attractive and repulsive forces between atoms when they share electrons is known as covalent bonding. Covalent bonding includes many kinds of interaction, including σ-bonding, π-bonding, metal-to-metal bonding, agostic interactions, and three-center two-electron bonds.
Capillary action	Capillary action, is the ability of a liquid to flow against gravity where liquid spontaneously rises in a narrow space such as a thin tube, or in porous materials such as paper or in some non-porous materials such as liquified carbon fibre. This effect can cause liquids to flow against the force of gravity or the magnetic field induction. It occurs because of inter-molecular attractive forces between the liquid and solid surrounding surfaces; If the diameter of the tube is sufficiently small, then the combination of surface tension (which is caused by cohesion within the liquid) and forces of adhesion between the liquid and container act to lift the liquid.
Surface tension	Surface tension is a property of the surface of a liquid that allows it to resi an external force. It is revealed, for example, in the floating of some objects on the surface of water, even though they are denser than water, and in the ability of some insects (e.g. water riders) to run on the water surface. This property is caused by cohesion of similar molecules, and is responsible for many of the behaviors of liquids.
Polar	The Global Geospace Science (GGS) Polar Satellite was a NASA science spacecraft designed to study the polar magnetosphere and aurora. It was launched into orbit in February 1996, and continued operations until the program was terminated in April 2008. The spacecraft remains in orbit, though it is now inactive. Polar is the sister ship to GGS Wind.
Chemical reaction	A chemical reaction is a process that leads to the transformation of one set of chemical substances to another. Chemical reactions can be either spontaneous, requiring no input of energy, or non-spontaneous, typically following the input of some type of energy, such as heat, light or electricity. Classically, chemical reactions encompass changes that strictly involve the motion of electrons in the forming and breaking of chemical bonds, although the general concept of a chemical reaction, in particular the notion of a chemical equation, is applicable to transformations of elementary particles (such as illustrated by Feynman diagrams), as well as nuclear reactions.
Enzyme	Enzymes ( ) are proteins that catalyze (i.e., increase the rates of) chemical reactions. In enzymatic reactions, the molecules at the beginning of the process, called substrates, are converted into different molecules, called products. Almost all chemical reactions in a biological cell need enzymes in order to occur at rates sufficient for life.
Macromolecule	A macromolecule is a very large molecule commonly created by polymerization of smaller subunits.

Visit Cram101.com for full Practice Exams

2. Environmental Systems

CHAPTER HIGHLIGHTS & NOTES: KEY TERMS, PEOPLE, PLACES, CONCEPTS

	In biochemistry, the term is applied to the four conventional biopolymers (nucleic acids, proteins, carbohydrates, and lipids), as well as non-polymeric molecules with large molecular mass such as macrocycles. The individual constituent molecules of macromolecules are called monomers (mono=single, meros=part).
Organic compound	An organic compound is any member of a large class of gaseous, liquid, or solid chemical compounds whose molecules contain carbon. For historical reasons discussed below, a few types of carbon-containing compounds such as carbides, carbonates, simple oxides of carbon (such as CO and CO_2), and cyanides, as well as the allotropes of carbon such as diamond and graphite, are considered inorganic. The distinction between 'organic' and 'inorganic' carbon compounds, while 'useful in organizing the vast subject of chemistry... is somewhat arbitrary'.
Polysaccharide	Polysaccharides are long carbohydrate molecules of repeated monomer units joined together by glycosidic bonds. They range in structure from linear to highly branched. Polysaccharides are often quite heterogeneous, containing slight modifications of the repeating unit.
Photon	In physics, a photon is an elementary particle, the quantum of light and all other forms of electromagnetic radiation, and the force carrier for the electromagnetic force. The effects of this force are easily observable at both the microscopic and macroscopic level, because the photon has no rest mass; this allows for interactions at long distances. Like all elementary particles, photons are currently best explained by quantum mechanics and exhibit wave-particle duality, exhibiting properties of both waves and particles.
Kinetic energy	The kinetic energy of an object is the energy which it possesses due to its motion. It is defined as the work needed to accelerate a body of a given mass from rest to its stated velocity. Having gained this energy during its acceleration, the body maintains this kinetic energy unless its speed changes.
Potential energy	In physics, potential energy is the energy of a body or a system due to the position of the body or the arrangement of the particles of the system. The SI unit for measuring work and energy is the Joule (symbol J). The term 'potential energy' was coined by the 19th century Scottish engineer and physicist William Rankine.
Chemical energy	In chemistry, Chemical energy is the potential of a chemical substan to undergo a transformation through a chemical reaction or, to transform other chemical substans.Template:Fusion Breaking or making of chemical bonds involves energy, which may be either absorbed or evolved from a chemical system. Energy that can be released (or absorbed) because of a reaction between a set of chemical substans is equal to the differen between the energy content of the products and the reactants. This change in energy is change in internal energy of a chemical reaction.
First law of thermodynamics	ImgProperty databaseimg

Visit Cram101.com for full Practice Exams

2. Environmental Systems

CHAPTER HIGHLIGHTS & NOTES: KEY TERMS, PEOPLE, PLACES, CONCEPTS

The first law of thermodynamics is a version of the law of conservation of energy, specialized for thermodynamical systems. It is usually formulated by stating that the change in the internal energy of a closed system is equal to the amount of heat supplied to the system, minus the amount of work performed by the system on its surroundings. The law of conservation of energy can be stated: The energy of an isolated system is constant.

Second law of thermodynamics

The second law of thermodynamics is an expression of the tendency that over time, differences in temperature, pressure, and chemical potential equilibrate in an isolated physical system. From the state of thermodynamic equilibrium, the law deduced the principle of the increase of entropy and explains the phenomenon of irreversibility in nature. The second law declares the impossibility of machines that generate usable energy from the abundant internal energy of nature by processes called perpetual motion of the second kind.

Energy quality

Energy quality is the contrast between different forms of energy, the different trophic levels in ecological systems and the propensity of energy to convert from one form to another. The concept refers to the empirical experience of the characteristics, or qualia, of different energy forms as they flow and transform. It appeals to our common perception of the heat value, versatility, and environmental performance of different energy forms and the way a small increment in energy flow can sometimes produce a large transformation effect on both energy physical state and energy.

Energy transformation

Energy transformation is the process of changing one form of energy to another. In physics, the term energy describes the capacity to produce certain changes within a system, without regard to limitations in transformation imposed by entropy. Changes in total energy of systems can only be accomplished by adding or subtracting energy from them, as energy is a quantity which is conserved, according to the first law of thermodynamics.

Available energy

In particle physics, the available energy is the energy in a particle collision available to produce new matter from the kinetic energy of the colliding particles. Since the conservation of momentum must be held, a system of two particles with a net momentum may not convert all their kinetic energy into mass - and thus the available energy is always less than or equal to the kinetic energy of the colliding particles. The available energy for a system of one stationary particle and one moving particle is defined as:

$$E_a = \sqrt{2m_t c^2 E_m + (m_t c^2)^2 + (m_k c^2)^2}$$

where m_t is the mass of the stationary target particle, m_k is the mass of the moving particle, E_m is the kinetic energy of the moving particle, and c is the speed of light..

Conversion

In chemistry, the phrase conversion has several meanings•specifically the property 'X' related to the yield 'Y' by multiplication with the selectivity 'S', i.e. the mathematical definition X(conversion) * S(selectivity) = Y(yield), all calculated on a molar basis; e.g.

Visit Cram101.com for full Practice Exams

2. Environmental Systems

CHAPTER HIGHLIGHTS & NOTES: KEY TERMS, PEOPLE, PLACES, CONCEPTS

in a certain reaction, 90% of substance A is converted (consumed), but only 80% of it is converted to the desired substance B and 20% to undesired by-products, so conversion of A is 90%, selectivity for B 80% and yield of substance B 72% (= 90% * 80%)•in a general sense the action of a chemical reaction, e.g. the conversion of molecule A to molecule B; note that in this general sense, conversion rate would be synonymous with reaction rate.

Open system

An open system is a system which continuously interacts with its environment. An open system should be contrasted with the concept of an isolated system which exchanges neither energy, matter,nor information with its environment.

The concept of an 'open system' was formalized within a framework that enabled one to interrelate the theory of the organism, thermodynamics, and evolutionary theory.

Systems analysis

Systems analysis is the study of sets of interacting entities, including computer systems analysis. This field is closely related to requirements analysis or operations research. It is also 'an explicit formal inquiry carried out to help someone (referred to as the decision maker) identify a better course of action and make a better decision than he might otherwise have made.'

The terms analysis and synthesis come from Greek where they mean respectively 'to take apart' and 'to put together'.

Energy flow

In ecology, energy flow, also called the calorific flow, rrs to the flow of energy through a food chain. In an ecosystem, ecologists seek to quantify the relative importance of different component species and feeding relationships.

A general energy flow scenario follows:•Solar energy is fixed by the photoautotrophs, called primary producers, like green plants.

Steady state

A system in a steady state has numerous properties that are unchanging in time. This implies that for any property p of the system, the partial derivative with respect to time is zero: $\frac{\partial p}{\partial t} = 0$

The concept of steady state has relevance in many fields, in particular thermodynamics and economics. Steady state is a more general situation than dynamic equilibrium.

Negative feedback loop

Negative feedback occurs when the result of a process influences the operation of the process itself in such a way as to reduce changes. Negative feedback tends to make a system self-regulating; it can produce stability and reduce the effect of fluctuations. Negative feedback loops where just the right amount of correction is applied in the most timely manner can be very stable, accurate, and responsive.

Visit Cram101.com for full Practice Exams

2. Environmental Systems

CHAPTER HIGHLIGHTS & NOTES: KEY TERMS, PEOPLE, PLACES, CONCEPTS

Sustainable management	Sustainable management takes the concepts from sustainability and synthesizes them with the concepts of management. Sustainability has three branches: the environment, the needs of present and future generations, and the economy. Using these branches, it creates the ability to keep a system running indefinitely without depleting resources, maintaining economic viability, and also nourishing the needs of the present and future generations.
Ozone layer	The ozone layer is a layer in Earth's atmosphere which contains relatively high concentrations of ozone (O_3). This layer absorbs 97-99% of the Sun's high frequency ultraviet light, which potentially damages the life forms on Earth. It is mainly located in the lower portion of the stratosphere from approximately 20 to 30 kilometres (12 to 19 mi) above Earth, though the thickness varies seasonally and geographically.
Catalyst	Catalysis is the change in rate of a chemical reaction due to the participation of a substance called a catalyst. Unlike other reagents that participate in the chemical reaction, a catalyst is not consumed by the reaction itself. A catalyst may participate in multiple chemical transformations.
Montreal Protocol	The Montreal Protocol on Substances That Deplete the Ozone Layer (a protocol to the Vienna Convention for the Protection of the Ozone Layer) is an international treaty designed to protect the ozone layer by phasing out the production of numerous substances believed to be responsible for ozone depletion. The treaty was opened for signature on September 16, 1987, and entered into force on January 1, 1989, followed by a first meeting in Helsinki, May 1989. Since then, it has undergone seven revisions, in 1990 (London), 1991 (Nairobi), 1992 (Copenhagen), 1993 (Bangkok), 1995 (Vienna), 1997 (Montreal), and 1999 (Beijing). It is believed that if the international agreement is adhered to, the ozone layer is expected to recover by 2050. Due to its widespread adoption and implementation it has been hailed as an example of exceptional international co-operation, with Kofi Annan quoted as saying that 'perhaps the single most successful international agreement to date has been the Montreal Protocol'.

Visit Cram101.com for full Practice Exams

2. Environmental Systems

CHAPTER QUIZ: KEY TERMS, PEOPLE, PLACES, CONCEPTS

1. An _____ is a system which continuously interacts with its environment. An _____ should be contrasted with the concept of an isolated system which exchanges neither energy, matter, nor information with its environment.

   The concept of an '_____' was formalized within a framework that enabled one to interrelate the theory of the organism, thermodynamics, and evolutionary theory.

   a. Output
   b. Limiting reagent
   c. Open system
   d. System size expansion

2. _____s ( ) are proteins that catalyze (i.e., increase the rates of) chemical reactions. In enzymatic reactions, the molecules at the beginning of the process, called substrates, are converted into different molecules, called products. Almost all chemical reactions in a biological cell need _____s in order to occur at rates sufficient for life.

   a. Enzyme
   b. Chemical state
   c. Chemical structure
   d. Chemical substance

3. A _____ is a very large molecule commonly created by polymerization of smaller subunits. In biochemistry, the term is applied to the four conventional biopolymers (nucleic acids, proteins, carbohydrates, and lipids), as well as non-polymeric molecules with large molecular mass such as macrocycles. The individual constituent molecules of _____s are called monomers (mono=single, meros=part).

   a. Macromonomer
   b. Melt flow index
   c. Macromolecule
   d. Molar mass distribution

4. . The _____ on Substances That Deplete the Ozone Layer (a protocol to the Vienna Convention for the Protection of the Ozone Layer) is an international treaty designed to protect the ozone layer by phasing out the production of numerous substances believed to be responsible for ozone depletion. The treaty was opened for signature on September 16, 1987, and entered into force on January 1, 1989, followed by a first meeting in Helsinki, May 1989. Since then, it has undergone seven revisions, in 1990 (London), 1991 (Nairobi), 1992 (Copenhagen), 1993 (Bangkok), 1995 (Vienna), 1997 (Montreal), and 1999 (Beijing). It is believed that if the international agreement is adhered to, the ozone layer is expected to recover by 2050. Due to its widespread adoption and implementation it has been hailed as an example of exceptional international co-operation, with Kofi Annan quoted as saying that 'perhaps the single most successful international agreement to date has been the _____'.

   a. Juglone
   b. Defoamer
   c. Detackifier

Visit Cram101.com for full Practice Exams

2. Environmental Systems

CHAPTER QUIZ: KEY TERMS, PEOPLE, PLACES, CONCEPTS

5. In the mathematical field of order theory, given two elements a and b of a partially ordered set, one says that b covers a, and writes a <: b or b :> a, if a < b and there is no element c such that a < c < b. In other words, b covers a if b is greater than a and minimal with this property, or equivalently if a is smaller than b and maximal with this property.

In a partially ordered set with least element 0, an _____ is an element that covers 0, i.e. an element that is minimal among the non-zero elements.

a. Atom
b. Ideal
c. Incidence algebra
d. Infimum

Visit Cram101.com for full Practice Exams

Visit Cram101.com for full Practice Exams

ANSWER KEY
2. Environmental Systems

1. c
2. a
3. c
4. d
5. a

You can take the complete Chapter Practice Test

for 2. Environmental Systems
on all key terms, persons, places, and concepts.

Online 99 Cents

http://www.epub89.16.23086.2.cram101.com/

Use www.Cram101.com for all your study needs

including Cram101's online interactive problem solving labs in

chemistry, statistics, mathematics, and more.

Visit Cram101.com for full Practice Exams

3. Ecosystem Ecology

CHAPTER OUTLINE: KEY TERMS, PEOPLE, PLACES, CONCEPTS

Ecosystem

Autotroph

Cellular respiration

Photosynthesis

Food chain

Food web

Heterotroph

Trophic level

Scavenger

Decomposers

Detritivore

Biomass

Biosphere

Biogeochemical cycle

Carbon cycle

Evapotranspiration

Precipitation

Transpiration

Ammonification

Nitrogen cycle

Nitrogen fixation

Visit Cram101.com for full Practice Exams

3. Ecosystem Ecology
CHAPTER OUTLINE: KEY TERMS, PEOPLE, PLACES, CONCEPTS

_____ | Algal bloom

_____ | Dead zone

_____ | Denitrification

_____ | Leaching

_____ | Phosphorus cycle

_____ | Sulfur dioxide

_____ | Restoration ecology

_____ | Ecosystem services

CHAPTER HIGHLIGHTS & NOTES: KEY TERMS, PEOPLE, PLACES, CONCEPTS

Ecosystem

An ecosystem is a community of living organisms (plants, animals and microbes) in conjunction with the nonliving components of their environment (things like air, water and mineral soil), interacting as a system. These components are regarded as linked together through nutrient cycles and energy flows. As ecosystems are defined by the network of interactions among organisms, and between organisms and their environment, they can come in any size but usually encompass specific, limited spaces (although some scientists say that the entire planet is an ecosystem).

Autotroph

An autotroph, is an organism that produces complex organic compounds (such as carbohydrates, fats, and proteins) from simple inorganic molecules using energy from light (by photosynthesis) or inorganic chemical reactions (chemosynthesis). They are the producers in a food chain, such as plants on land or algae in water. They are able to make their own food and can fix carbon.

Cellular respiration

Cellular respiration is the set of the metabolic reactions and processes that take place in the cells of organisms to convert biochemical energy from nutrients into adenosine triphosphate (ATP), and then release waste products. The reactions involved in respiration are catabolic reactions that involve the redox reaction (oxidation of one molecule and the reduction of another). Respiration is one of the key ways a cell gains useful energy to fuel cellular changes.

Visit Cram101.com for full Practice Exams

3. Ecosystem Ecology

CHAPTER HIGHLIGHTS & NOTES: KEY TERMS, PEOPLE, PLACES, CONCEPTS

Photosynthesis	Photosynthesis is a chemical process that converts carbon dioxide into organic compounds, especially sugars, using the energy from sunlight. Photosynthesis occurs in plants, algae, and many species of bacteria, but not in archaea. Photosynthetic organisms are called photoautotrophs, since they can create their own food.
Food chain	A food chain is somewhat a linear sequence of links in a food web starting from a trophic species that eats no other species in the web and ends at a trophic species that is eaten by no other species in the web. A food chain differs from a food web, because the complex polyphagous network of feeding relations are aggregated into trophic species and the chain only follows linear monophagous pathways. A common metric used to quantify food web trophic structure is food chain length.
Food web	A food web depicts feeding connections (what eats what) in an ecological community. Ecologists can broadly lump all life forms into one of two categories called trophic levels: 1) the autotrophs, and 2) the heterotrophs. To maintain their bodies, grow, develop, and to reproduce, autotrophs produce organic matter from inorganic substances, including both minerals and gases such as carbon dioxide.
Heterotroph	A heterotroph is an organism that cannot fix carbon and uses organic carbon for growth. This contrasts with autotrophs, such as plants and algae, which can use energy from sunlight (photoautotrophs) or inorganic compounds (lithoautotrophs) to produce organic compounds such as carbohydrates, fats, and proteins from inorganic carbon dioxide. These reduced carbon compounds can be used as an energy source by the autotroph and provide the energy in food consumed by heterotrophs.
Trophic level	The trophic level of an organism is the position it occupies in a food chain. A food chain represents a succession of organisms that eat another organism and are, in turn, eaten themselves. The number of steps an organism is from the start of the chain is a measure of its trophic level.
Scavenger	Scavenging is both a carnivorous and herbivorous feeding behaviour in which individual scavengers search out dead animal (corpses or carrion) and dead plant biomass on which to feed . The eating of carrion from the same species is referred to as cannibalism. Scavengers play an important role in the ecosystem by contributing to the decomposition of dead animal and plant material.
Decomposers	Decomposers are organisms that break down dead or decaying organisms, and in doing so carry out the natural process of decomposition. Like herbivores and predators, decomposers are heterotrophic, meaning that they use organic substrates to get their energy, carbon and nutrients for growth and development. Decomposers can break down cells of other organisms using biochemical reactions that convert the prey tissue into metabolically useful chemical products, without need for internal digestion.

Visit Cram101.com for full Practice Exams

3. Ecosystem Ecology

CHAPTER HIGHLIGHTS & NOTES: KEY TERMS, PEOPLE, PLACES, CONCEPTS

Detritivore	Detritivores, also known as detritophages or detritus feeders or detritus eaters or saprophages, are heterotrophs that obtain nutrients by consuming detritus (decomposing organic matter). By doing so, they contribute to decomposition and the nutrient cycles. They should be distinguished from other decomposers, such as many species of bacteria, fungi and protists, unable to ingest discrete lumps of matter, instead live by absorbing and metabolising on a molecular scale.
Biomass	Biomass, in ecology, is the mass of living biological organisms in a given area or ecosystem at a given time. Biomass can refer to species biomass, which is the mass of one or more species, or to community biomass, which is the mass of all species in the community. It can include microorganisms, plants or animals.
Biosphere	The biosphere is the global sum of all ecosystems. It can also be called the zone of life on Earth, a closed (apart from solar and cosmic radiation), and self-regulating system. From the broadest biophysiological point of view, the biosphere is the global ecological system integrating all living beings and their relationships, including their interaction with the elements of the lithosphere, hydrosphere, and atmosphere.
Biogeochemical cycle	In geography and Earth science, a biogeochemical cycle is a pathway by which a chemical element or molecule moves through both biotic (biosphere) and abiotic (lithosphere, atmosphere, and hydrosphere) compartments of Earth. A cycle is a series of change which comes back to the starting point and which can be repeated. The term 'biogeochemical' tells us that biological, geological and chemical factors are all involved.
Carbon cycle	The carbon cycle is the biogeochemical cycle by which carbon is exchanged among the biosphere, pedosphere, geosphere, hydrosphere, and atmosphere of the Earth. Along with the nitrogen cycle and the water cycle, the carbon cycle comprises a sequence of events that are key to making the Earth capable of sustaining life; it describes the movement of carbon as it is recycled and reused throughout the biosphere. The global carbon budget is the balance of the exchanges (incomes and losses) of carbon between the carbon reservoirs or between one specific loop (e.g., atmosphere ↔ biosphere) of the carbon cycle.
Evapotranspiration	Evapotranspiration is the sum of evaporation and plant transpiration from the Earth's land surface to atmosphere. Evaporation accounts for the movement of water to the air from sources such as the soil, canopy interception, and waterbodies. Transpiration accounts for the movement of water within a plant and the subsequent loss of water as vapor through stomata in its leaves.
Precipitation	Precipitation is the formation of a solid in a solution or inside another solid during a chemical reaction or by diffusion in a solid. When the reaction occurs in a liquid, the solid formed is called the Precipitate, or when compacted by a centrifuge, a pellet.

Visit Cram101.com for full Practice Exams

3. Ecosystem Ecology

CHAPTER HIGHLIGHTS & NOTES: KEY TERMS, PEOPLE, PLACES, CONCEPTS

Transpiration	Transpiration is a process similar to evaporation. It is a part of the water cycle, and it is the loss of water vapor from parts of plants (similar to sweating), especially in leaves but also in stems, flowers and roots. Leaf surfaces are dotted with openings which are collectively called stomata, and in most plants they are more numerous on the undersides of the foliage.
Ammonification	The nitrogen cycle is the process by which nitrogen is converted between its various chemical forms. This transformation can be carried out through both biological and physical processes. Important processes in the nitrogen cycle include fixation, ammonification, nitrification, and denitrification.
	Ammonification or Mineralization is performed by bacteria to convert the ammonia to ammonium. Nitrification can then occur to convert the ammonium to nitrite and nitrate. Nitrate can be returned to the euphotic zone by vertical mixing and upwelling where it can be taken up by phytoplankton to continue the cycle. N_2 can be returned to the atmosphere through denitrification.
Nitrogen cycle	The nitrogen cycle is the process by which nitrogen is converted between its various chemical forms. This transformation can be carried out via both biological and non-biological processes. Important processes in the nitrogen cycle include fixation, mineralization, nitrification, and denitrification.
Nitrogen fixation	Nitrogen fixation is a process, biological, abiotic, or synthetic by which nitrogen (N_2) in the atmosphere is converted into ammonia (NH_3). Atmospheric nitrogen or elemental nitrogen (N_2) is relatively inert: it does not easily react with other chemicals to form new compounds. Fixation processes free up the nitrogen atoms from their diatomic form (N_2) to be used in other ways.
Algal bloom	An algal bloom is a rapid increase or accumulation in the population of algae in an aquatic system. Algal blooms may occur in freshwater as well as marine environments. Typically, only one or a small number of phytoplankton species are involved, and some blooms may be recognized by discoloration of the water resulting from the high density of pigmented cells.
Dead zone	Dead zones are hypoxic (low-oxygen) areas in the world's oceans, the observed incidences of which have been increasing since oceanographers began noting them in the 1970s. These occur near inhabited coastlines, where aquatic life is most concentrated. (The vast middle portions of the oceans which naturally have little life are not considered 'dead zones'). The term can also be applied to the identical phenomenon in large lakes.
Denitrification	Denitrification is a microbially facilitated process of nitrate reduction that may ultimately produce molecular nitrogen (N_2) through a series of intermediate gaseous nitrogen oxide products.
	This respiratory process reduces oxidized forms of nitrogen in response to the oxidation of an electron donor such as organic matter.

Visit Cram101.com for full Practice Exams

3. Ecosystem Ecology

CHAPTER HIGHLIGHTS & NOTES: KEY TERMS, PEOPLE, PLACES, CONCEPTS

Leaching

Leaching Many Biological organic and inorganic substances occur in a mixture of different components in a solid. In order to separate the desired solute constituent or remove an undesirable solute component from the solid phase, the solid is brought into contact with a liquid. The solid and liquid are in contact and the solute or solutes can diffuse from the solid into the solvent, resulting in separation of the components originally in the solid.

Phosphorus cycle

The phosphorus cycle is the biogeochemical cycle that describes the movement of phosphorus through the lithosphere, hydrosphere, and biosphere. Unlike many other biogeochemical cycles, the atmosphere does not play a significant role in the movement of phosphorus, because phosphorus and phosphorus-based compounds are usually solids at the typical ranges of temperature and pressure found on Earth. The production of phosphine gas occurs only in specialized, local conditions.

Sulfur dioxide

Sulfur dioxide is the chemical compound with the formula SO_2. It is a toxic gas with a pungent, irritating smell, that is released by volcanoes and in various industrial processes. Since coal and petroleum often contain sulfur compounds, their combustion generates sulfur dioxide unless the sulfur compounds are removed before burning the fuel.

Restoration ecology

Restoration ecology is the scientific study and practice of renewing and restoring degraded, damaged, or destroyed ecosystems and habitats in the environment by active human intervention and action. Restoration ecology emerged as a separate field in ecology in the 1980s.

History

Land managers, laypeople, and stewards have been practicing restoration for many hundreds, if not thousands of years, yet the scientific field of 'restoration ecology' was first identified and coined in the late 1980s by John Aber and William Jordan.

Ecosystem services

Humankind benefits from a multitude of resources and processes that are supplied by natural ecosystems. Collectively, these benefits are known as ecosystem services and include products like clean drinking water and processes such as the decomposition of wastes. While scientists and environmentalists have discussed ecosystem services for decades, these services were popularized and their definitions formalized by the United Nations 2004 Millennium Ecosystem Assessment (MA), a four-year study involving more than 1,300 scientists worldwide.

Visit Cram101.com for full Practice Exams

3. Ecosystem Ecology

CHAPTER QUIZ: KEY TERMS, PEOPLE, PLACES, CONCEPTS

1. An _____ is a community of living organisms (plants, animals and microbes) in conjunction with the nonliving components of their environment (things like air, water and mineral soil), interacting as a system. These components are regarded as linked together through nutrient cycles and energy flows. As _____s are defined by the network of interactions among organisms, and between organisms and their environment, they can come in any size but usually encompass specific, limited spaces (although some scientists say that the entire planet is an _____).

   a. Odyssey
   b. Endangered Species Act
   c. Ecosystem
   d. Absent-minded professor

2. _____ is a chemical process that converts carbon dioxide into organic compounds, especially sugars, using the energy from sunlight. _____ occurs in plants, algae, and many species of bacteria, but not in archaea. Photosynthetic organisms are called photoautotrophs, since they can create their own food.

   a. Photosynthesis
   b. 1,3-Bisphosphoglyceric acid
   c. Blood oxygen level
   d. Citric acid cycle

3. _____ is the chemical compound with the formula SO2. It is a toxic gas with a pungent, irritating smell, that is released by volcanoes and in various industrial processes. Since coal and petroleum often contain sulfur compounds, their combustion generates _____ unless the sulfur compounds are removed before burning the fuel.

   a. Sulfur dioxide
   b. Rarobacteraceae
   c. Rathayibacter
   d. Rathayibacter tritici

4. The _____ of an organism is the position it occupies in a food chain. A food chain represents a succession of organisms that eat another organism and are, in turn, eaten themselves. The number of steps an organism is from the start of the chain is a measure of its _____.

   a. profundal zone
   b. population biology
   c. Seral community
   d. Trophic level

5. . _____ is the set of the metabolic reactions and processes that take place in the cells of organisms to convert biochemical energy from nutrients into adenosine triphosphate (ATP), and then release waste products. The reactions involved in respiration are catabolic reactions that involve the redox reaction (oxidation of one molecule and the reduction of another). Respiration is one of the key ways a cell gains useful energy to fuel cellular changes.

   a. Beta oxidation

Visit Cram101.com for full Practice Exams

3. Ecosystem Ecology

CHAPTER QUIZ: KEY TERMS, PEOPLE, PLACES, CONCEPTS

b. 1,3-Bisphosphoglyceric acid

c. Cellular respiration

d. Citric acid cycle

Visit Cram101.com for full Practice Exams

Visit Cram101.com for full Practice Exams

ANSWER KEY
3. Ecosystem Ecology

1. c

2. a

3. a

4. d

5. c

You can take the complete Chapter Practice Test

for 3. Ecosystem Ecology
on all key terms, persons, places, and concepts.

Online 99 Cents

http://www.epub89.16.23086.3.cram101.com/

Use www.Cram101.com for all your study needs

including Cram101's online interactive problem solving labs in

chemistry, statistics, mathematics, and more.

Visit Cram101.com for full Practice Exams

4. Global Climates and Biomes

CHAPTER OUTLINE: KEY TERMS, PEOPLE, PLACES, CONCEPTS

Exosphere

Mesosphere

Stratosphere

Thermosphere

Troposphere

Ozone layer

Albedo

Coriolis effect

Hadley cell

Intertropical Convergence Zone

Population size

Trade wind

Solstice

Tropic of Cancer

Tropic of Capricorn

Westerlies

Current

Thermohaline circulation

Upwelling

Rain shadow

Biome

Visit Cram101.com for full Practice Exams

4. Global Climates and Biomes
CHAPTER OUTLINE: KEY TERMS, PEOPLE, PLACES, CONCEPTS

Growing season

Permafrost

Tundra

Temperate rainforest

Tropical rainforest

Benthic zone

Limnetic zone

Littoral zone

Phytoplankton

Profundal zone

Wetland

Coral reef

Intertidal zone

Salt marsh

Mangrove

Coral bleaching

Starfish

Chemosynthesis

Photic zone

Shade-grown coffee

Visit Cram101.com for full Practice Exams

4. Global Climates and Biomes

Exosphere	The exosphere is a thin, atmosphere-like volume surrounding a planetary body where molecules are gravitationally bound to that body, but where the density is too low for them to behave as a gas by colliding with each other. In the case of bodies with substantial atmospheres, such as the Earth's atmosphere, the exosphere is the uppermost layer, where the atmosphere thins out and merges with interplanetary space. It is located directly above the Thermosphere.
Mesosphere	The mesosphere refers to the mantle in the region between the asthenosphere and the outer core. The upper boundary is defined as the sharp increase in seismic wave velocities and density at a depth of 660 km. As depth increases, pressure builds and forces atoms into a denser, more rigid structure; thus the difference between mesosphere and asthenosphere is likely due to density and rigidity differences, that is, physical factors, and not to any difference in chemical composition.
Stratosphere	The stratosphere is the second major layer of Earth's atmosphere, just above the troposphere, and below the mesosphere. It is stratified in temperature, with warmer layers higher up and cooler layers farther down. This is in contrast to the troposphere near the Earth's surface, which is cooler higher up and warmer farther down.
Thermosphere	The thermosphere is the layer of the Earth's atmosphere directly above the mesosphere and directly below the exosphere. Within this layer, ultraviolet radiation causes ionization. The International Space Station has a stable orbit within the middle of the thermosphere, between 320 and 380 kilometres (200 and 240 mi).
Troposphere	The troposphere is the lowest portion of Earth's atmosphere. It contains approximately 80% of the atmosphere's mass and 99% of its water vapor and aerosols. The average depth of the troposphere is approximately 17 km (11 mi) in the middle latitudes.
Ozone layer	The ozone layer is a layer in Earth's atmosphere which contains relatively high concentrations of ozone (O_3). This layer absorbs 97-99% of the Sun's high frequency ultraviet light, which potentially damages the life forms on Earth. It is mainly located in the lower portion of the stratosphere from approximately 20 to 30 kilometres (12 to 19 mi) above Earth, though the thickness varies seasonally and geographically.
Albedo	Albedo or reflection coefficient, derived from Latin albedo 'whiteness' (or reflected sunlight), in turn from albus 'white', is the diffuse reflectivity or reflecting power of a surface. It is defined as the ratio of reflected radiation from the surface to incident radiation upon it. Being a dimensionless fraction, it may also be expressed as a percentage, and is measured on a scale from zero for no reflecting power of a perfectly black surface, to 1 for perfect reflection of a white surface.
Coriolis effect	In physics, the Coriolis effect is a deflection of moving objects when they are viewed in a rotating referen frame. In a referen frame with clockwise rotation, the deflection is to the left of the motion of the object; in one with counter-clockwise rotation, the deflection is to the right.

Visit Cram101.com for full Practice Exams

4. Global Climates and Biomes

CHAPTER HIGHLIGHTS & NOTES: KEY TERMS, PEOPLE, PLACES, CONCEPTS

The mathematical expression for the Coriolis for appeared in an 1835 paper by French scientist Gaspard-Gustave Coriolis, in connection with the theory of water wheels, and also in the tidal equations of Pierre-Simon Lapla in 1778. And even earlier, Italian scientists Giovanni Battista Riccioli and his assistant Fransco Maria Grimaldi described the effect in connection with artillery in the 1651 Almagestum Novum, writing that rotation of the Earth should cause a cannon ball fired to the north to deflect to the east.

Hadley cell

The Hadley cell, is a tropical atmospheric circulation that is defined by the average over longitude, which features rising motion near the equator, poleward flow 10-15 kilometers above the surface, descending motion in the subtropics, and equatorward flow near the surface. This circulation is intimately related to the trade winds, tropical rainbelts & hurricanes, subtropical deserts and the jet streams.

There are three primary circulation cells.

Intertropical Convergence Zone

The Intertropical Convergence Zone known by sailors as the doldrums, is the area encircling the earth near the equator where the northeast and southeast trade winds come together.

The ITCZ was originally identified from the 1920s to the 1940s as the 'Intertropical Front' (ITF), but after the recognition in the 1940s and 1950s of the significance of wind field convergence in tropical weather production, the term 'ITCZ' was then applied. When it lies near the equator, it is called the near-equatorial trough.

Population size

In population genetics and population ecology, population size is the number of individual organisms in a population.

The effective population size is defined as 'the number of breeding individuals in an idealized population that would show the same amount of dispersion of allele frequencies under random genetic drift or the same amount of inbreeding as the population under consideration.' N_e is usually less than N (the absolute population size) and this has important applications in conservation genetics.

Small population size results in increased genetic drift.

Trade wind

The trade winds (also called trades) are the prevailing pattern of easterly surface winds found in the tropics, within the lower portion of the Earth's atmosphere, in the lower section of the troposphere near the Earth's equator. The trade winds blow predominantly from the northeast in the Northern Hemisphere and from the southeast in the Southern Hemisphere, strengthening during the winter and when the Arctic oscillation is in its warm phase.

Visit Cram101.com for full Practice Exams

4. Global Climates and Biomes

Solstice	A solstice is an astronomical event that happens twice each year when the Sun reaches its highest position in the sky as seen from the North or South Pole. The word solstice is derived from the Latin sol (sun) and sistere (to stand still), because at the solstices, the Sun stands still in declination; that is, the seasonal movement of the Sun's path comes to a stop before reversing direction. The solstices, together with the equinoxes, are connected with the seasons.
Tropic of Cancer	? (Prime Meridian) The Tropic of Cancer, also referred to as the Northern tropic, is the circle of latitude on the Earth that marks the most northerly position at which the Sun may appear directly overhead at its zenith. This event occurs once per year, at the time of the June solstice, when the Northern Hemisphere is tilted toward the Sun to its maximum extent. Its Southern Hemisphere counterpart, marking the most southerly position at which the Sun may appear directly overhead, is the Tropic of Capricorn.
Tropic of Capricorn	? (Prime Meridian) The Tropic of Capricorn, marks the most southerly latitude at which the Sun can appear directly overhead. This event occurs at the December solstice, when the southern hemisphere is tilted towards the Sun to its maximum extent. Tropic of Capricorn is one of the five major circles of latitude that mark maps of the Earth.
Westerlies	The Westerlies, anti-trades, or Prevailing Westerlies, are the prevailing winds in the middle latitudes between 30 and 60 degrees latitude, blowing from the high pressure area in the horse latitudes towards the poles. These prevailing winds blow from the west to the east, and steer extratropical cyclones in this general manner. Tropical cyclones which cross the subtropical ridge axis into the Westerlies recurve due to the increased westerly flow.
Current	In mathematics, more particularly in functional analysis, differential topology, and geometric measure theory, a k-current in the sense of Georges de Rham is a functional on the space of compactly supported differential k-forms, on a smooth manifold M. Formally currents behave like Schwartz distributions on a space of differential forms. In a geometric setting, they can represent integration over a submanifold, generalizing the Dirac delta function, or more generally even directional derivatives of delta functions (multipoles) spread out along subsets of M. Let $\Omega_c^m(\mathbb{R}^n)$ denote the space of smooth m-forms with compact support on $\mathbb{R}^n$. A current is a linear functional on $\Omega_c^m(\mathbb{R}^n)$ which is continuous in the sense of distributions.
Thermohaline circulation	The term thermohaline circulation refers to the part of the large-scale ocean circulation that is driven by global density gradients created by surface heat and freshwater fluxes.

Visit Cram101.com for full Practice Exams

4. Global Climates and Biomes

CHAPTER HIGHLIGHTS & NOTES: KEY TERMS, PEOPLE, PLACES, CONCEPTS

	Wind-driven surface currents (such as the Gulf Stream) head polewards from the equatorial Atlantic Ocean, cooling all the while and eventually sinking at high latitudes (forming North Atlantic Deep Water). This dense water then flows into the ocean basins.
Upwelling	Upwelling is an oceanographic phenomenon that involves wind-driven motion of dense, cooler, and usually nutrient-rich water towards the ocean surface, replacing the warmer, usually nutrient-depleted surface water. The increased availability in upwelling regions results in high levels of primary productivity and thus fishery production. Approximately 25% of the total global marine fish catches come from five upwellings that occupy only 5% of the total ocean area.
Rain shadow	A rain shadow is a dry area on the lee side of a mountainous area. The mountains block the passage of rain-producing weather systems, casting a 'shadow' of dryness behind them. As shown by the diagram to the right, the warm moist air is 'pulled' by the prevailing winds over a mountain.
Biome	Biomes are climatically and geographically defined as similar climatic conditions on the Earth, such as communities of plants, animals, and soil organisms, and are often referred to as ecosystems. Some parts of the earth have more or less the same kind of abiotic and biotic factors spread over a large area, creating a typical ecosystem over that area. Such major ecosystems are termed as biomes.
Growing season	In botany, horticulture, and agriculture the growing season is the period of each year when native plants and ornamental plants grow; and when crops can be grown. The growing season is usually determined by climate and elevation, and in horticulture and agriculture the plant-crop selection. Depending on the location, temperature, daylight hours (photoperiod), and rainfall, may all be critical environmental factors.
Permafrost	In geology, permafrost is soil at or below the freezing point of water 0 °C (32 °F) for two or more years. Most permafrost is located in high latitudes (i.e. land close to the North and South poles), but alpine permafrost may exist at high altitudes in much lower latitudes. Ground ice is not always present, as may be in the case of nonporous bedrock, but it frequently occurs and it may be in amounts exceeding the potential hydraulic saturation of the ground material.
Tundra	In physical geography, tundra is a biome where the tree growth is hindered by low temperatures and short growing seasons. The term tundra comes through Russian тундра from the Kildin Sami word tundâr 'uplands,' 'treeless mountain tract.' There are three types of tundra: Arctic tundra, alpine tundra, and Antarctic tundra. In tundra, the vegetation is composed of dwarf shrubs, sedges and grasses, mosses, and lichens.
Temperate rainforest	Temperate rainforests are coniferous or broadleaf forests that occur in the temperate zone and receive high rainfall.

Visit Cram101.com for full Practice Exams

4. Global Climates and Biomes

CHAPTER HIGHLIGHTS & NOTES: KEY TERMS, PEOPLE, PLACES, CONCEPTS

For temperate rain forests of North America, Alaback's definition is widely recognized:•Annual precipitation 200-400 cm•Mean annual temperature between 4°C and 12°C. (39° and 54° Fahrenheit)

However, required annual precipitation depends on factors such as distribution of rainfall over the year, temperatures over the year and fog presence, and definitions in other countries differ considerably. For example, Australian definitions are ecological-structural rather than climatic:•Closed canopy of trees excludes at least 70% of the sky•Forest is composed mainly of tree species which do not require fire for regeneration, but with seedlings able to regenerate under shade and in natural openings

The latter would, for example, exclude a part of the temperate rain forests of western North America, as Coast Douglas-fir, one of its dominant tree species, requires stand-destroying disturbance to initiate a new cohort of seedlings.

Tropical rainforest	A tropical rainforest is a place roughly within 28 degrees north or south of the equator. They are found in Asia, Australia, Africa, South America, Central America, Mexico and on many of the Pacific Islands. Within the World Wildlife Fund's biome classification, tropical rainforests are thought to be a type of tropical wet forest (or tropical moist broadleaf forest) and may also be referred to as lowland equatorial evergreen rainforest.
Benthic zone	The benthic zone is the ecological region at the lowest level of a body of water such as an ocean or a lake, including the sediment surface and some sub-surface layers. Organisms living in this zone are called benthos. They generally live in close relationship with the substrate bottom; many such organisms are permanently attached to the bottom.
Limnetic zone	The limnetic zone is the well-lit, open surface waters in a lake, away from the shore. The vegetation of the littoral zone surrounds this expanse of open water and it is above the profundal zone. This is the main photosynthetic body of the lake.
Littoral zone	The littoral zone is that part of a sea, lake or river that is close to the shore. In coastal environments the littoral zone extends from the high water mark, which is rarely inundated, to shoreline areas that are permanently submerged. It always includes this intertidal zone and is often used to mean the same as the intertidal zone.
Phytoplankton	Phytoplankton are the autotrophic component of the plankton community. Most phytoplankton are too small to be individually seen with the unaided eye.

Visit Cram101.com for full Practice Exams

4. Global Climates and Biomes

CHAPTER HIGHLIGHTS & NOTES: KEY TERMS, PEOPLE, PLACES, CONCEPTS

Profundal zone	The profundal zone is a very cold and ordinary zone, such as an ocean or a lake, located below the range of effective light penetration. This is typically below the thermocline, the vertical zone in the water through which temperature drops rapidly. The lack of light in the profundal zone determines the type of biological community that can live in this region, which is distinctly different from the community in the overlying waters.
Wetland	A wetland is a land area that is saturated with water, either permanently or seasonally, such that it takes on the characteristics of a distinct ecosystem. Primarily, the factor that distinguishes wetlands from other land forms or water bodies is the characteristic vegetation that is adapted to its unique soil conditions: Wetlands consist primarily of hydric soil, which supports aquatic plants.
	The water found in wetlands can be saltwater, freshwater, or brackish.
Coral reef	Coral reefs are underwater structures made from calcium carbonate secreted by corals. Corals are colonies of tiny living animals found in marine waters that contain few nutrients. Most coral reefs are built from stony corals, which in turn consist of polyps that cluster in groups.
Intertidal zone	The intertidal zone is the area that is above water at low tide and under water at high tide (for example, the area between tide marks). This area can include many different types of habitats, with many types of animals like starfish, sea urchins, and some species of coral. The well known area also includes steep rocky cliffs, sandy beaches, or wetlands (e.g., vast mudflats).
Salt marsh	A salt marsh, is a coastal ecosystem in the upper coastal intertidal zone between land and open salt water or brackish water that is regularly flooded by the tides. It is dominated by dense stands of salt-tolerant plants such as herbs, grasses, or low shrubs. These plants are terrestrial in origin and are essential to the stability of the salt marsh in trapping and binding sediments.
Mangrove	Mangroves are various kinds of trees up to medium height and shrubs that grow in saline coastal sediment habitats in the tropics and subtropics - mainly between latitudes 25° N and 25° S. The remaining mangrove forest areas of the world in 2000 was 53,190 square miles (137,760 km²) spanning 118 countries and territories. The word is used in at least three senses: (1) most broadly to refer to the habitat and entire plant assemblage or mangal, for which the terms mangrove forest biome, mangrove swamp and mangrove forest are also used, (2) to refer to all trees and large shrubs in the mangrove swamp, and (3) narrowly to refer to the mangrove family of plants, the Rhizophoraceae, or even more specifically just to mangrove trees of the genus Rhizophora. The term 'mangrove' comes to English from Spanish (perhaps by way of Portuguese), and is of Caribbean origin, likely Taíno.
Coral bleaching	Coral bleaching is the loss of intracellular endosymbionts (Symbiodinium, also known as zooxanthellae) through either expulsion or loss of algal pigmentation. The corals that form the structure of the great reef ecosystems of tropical seas depend upon a symbiotic relationship with unicellular flagellate protozoa that are photosynthetic and live within their tissues.

Visit Cram101.com for full Practice Exams

4. Global Climates and Biomes

CHAPTER HIGHLIGHTS & NOTES: KEY TERMS, PEOPLE, PLACES, CONCEPTS

Starfish	Starfish are echinoderms belonging to the class Asteroidea. The names 'starfish' and 'sea star' essentially refer to members of the class Asteroidea. However, common usage frequently finds these names also applied to ophiuroids, which are correctly referred to as 'brittle stars' or 'basket stars'.
Chemosynthesis	In biochemistry, chemosynthesis is the biological conversion of one or more carbon molecules (usually carbon dioxide or methane) and nutrients into organic matter using the oxidation of inorganic molecules (e.g. hydrogen gas, hydrogen sulfide) or methane as a source of energy, rather than sunlight, as in photosynthesis. Chemoautotrophs, organisms that obtain carbon through chemosynthesis, are phylogenetically diverse, but groups that include conspicuous or biogeochemically-important taxa include the sulfur-oxidizing gamma and epsilon proteobacteria, the Aquificaeles, the Methanogenic archaea and the neutrophilic iron-oxidizing bacteria. Many microorganisms in dark regions of the oceans also use chemosynthesis to produce biomass from single carbon molecules.
Photic zone	The photic zone is exposed to sufficient sunlight for photosynthesis to occur. The depth of the photic zone can be affected greatly by seasonal turbidity. It extends from the atmosphere-water interface downwards to a depth where light intensity falls to one percent of that at the surface, called the euphotic depth.
Shade-grown coffee	Shade-grown coffee is a form of the beverage produced from coffee plants grown under a canopy of trees. Because it incorporates principles of natural ecology to promote natural ecological relationships, shade-grown coffee can be considered an offshoot of agricultural permaculture. History Most of the original coffee trees brought to the New World from European countries would burn in the sun, which made shade necessary for growth.

Visit Cram101.com for full Practice Exams

4. Global Climates and Biomes

CHAPTER QUIZ: KEY TERMS, PEOPLE, PLACES, CONCEPTS

1. A _____ is a place roughly within 28 degrees north or south of the equator. They are found in Asia, Australia, Africa, South America, Central America, Mexico and on many of the Pacific Islands. Within the World Wildlife Fund's biome classification, _____s are thought to be a type of tropical wet forest (or tropical moist broadleaf forest) and may also be referred to as lowland equatorial evergreen rainforest.

   a. temperate deciduous forest
   b. Tropical rainforest
   c. Juglone
   d. Gibbons v. Ogden

2. The _____, is a tropical atmospheric circulation that is defined by the average over longitude, which features rising motion near the equator, poleward flow 10-15 kilometers above the surface, descending motion in the subtropics, and equatorward flow near the surface. This circulation is intimately related to the trade winds, tropical rainbelts & hurricanes, subtropical deserts and the jet streams.

   There are three primary circulation cells.

   a. Hawaiian-Emperor seamount chain
   b. High capacity oceanographic lithium battery pack
   c. Hadley cell
   d. Kodiak-Bowie Seamount chain

3. The _____ is a layer in Earth's atmosphere which contains relatively high concentrations of ozone (O_3). This layer absorbs 97-99% of the Sun's high frequency ultraviet light, which potentially damages the life forms on Earth. It is mainly located in the lower portion of the stratosphere from approximately 20 to 30 kilometres (12 to 19 mi) above Earth, though the thickness varies seasonally and geographically.

   a. Ozone Mapping and Profiler Suite
   b. Ozone layer
   c. Odyssey
   d. Endangered Species Act

4. The _____ is a thin, atmosphere-like volume surrounding a planetary body where molecules are gravitationally bound to that body, but where the density is too low for them to behave as a gas by colliding with each other. In the case of bodies with substantial atmospheres, such as the Earth's atmosphere, the _____ is the uppermost layer, where the atmosphere thins out and merges with interplanetary space. It is located directly above the Thermosphere.

   a. Exosphere
   b. Odyssey
   c. Endangered Species Act
   d. United Nations Framework Convention on Climate Change

Visit Cram101.com for full Practice Exams

4. Global Climates and Biomes

5. A _____ is a land area that is saturated with water, either permanently or seasonally, such that it takes on the characteristics of a distinct ecosystem. Primarily, the factor that distinguishes _____s from other land forms or water bodies is the characteristic vegetation that is adapted to its unique soil conditions: _____s consist primarily of hydric soil, which supports aquatic plants.

The water found in _____s can be saltwater, freshwater, or brackish.

a. Whale fall
b. Wetland
c. littoral
d. brackish

Visit Cram101.com for full Practice Exams

ANSWER KEY
4. Global Climates and Biomes

1. b
2. c
3. b
4. a
5. b

You can take the complete Chapter Practice Test

for 4. Global Climates and Biomes
on all key terms, persons, places, and concepts.

Online 99 Cents

http://www.epub89.16.23086.4.cram101.com/

Use www.Cram101.com for all your study needs

including Cram101's online interactive problem solving labs in

chemistry, statistics, mathematics, and more.

Visit Cram101.com for full Practice Exams

5. Evolution of Biodiversity

CHAPTER OUTLINE: KEY TERMS, PEOPLE, PLACES, CONCEPTS

Biodiversity

Species diversity

Species evenness

Species richness

Recombination

Domestication

Roundup

Charles Darwin

Allopatric speciation

Sympatric speciation

Extinction

Lake Tanganyika

Genetically modified organism

Species distribution

Fossil

Polar

Biodiversity hotspot

Visit Cram101.com for full Practice Exams

5. Evolution of Biodiversity

CHAPTER HIGHLIGHTS & NOTES: KEY TERMS, PEOPLE, PLACES, CONCEPTS

Biodiversity	Biodiversity is the degree of variation of life forms within a given species, ecosystem, biome, or an entire planet. Biodiversity is a measure of the health of ecosystems. Biodiversity is in part a function of climate.
Species diversity	Species diversity is the effective number of different species that are represented in a collection of individuals (a dataset). The effective number of species refers to the number of equally-abundant species needed to obtain the same mean proportional species abundance as that observed in the dataset of interest . Species diversity consists of two components, species richness and species evenness.
Species evenness	Species evenness refers to how close in numbers each species in an environment are. Mathematically it is defined as a diversity index, a measure of biodiversity which quantifies how equal the community is numerically. So if there are 40 foxes, and 1000 dogs, the community is not very even.
Species richness	Species richness is the number of different species in a given area. It is represented in equation form as S. Species richness is the fundamental unit in which to assess the homogeneity of an environment. Typically, species richness is used in conservation studies to determine the sensitivity of ecosystems and their resident species. The actual number of species calculated alone is largely an arbitrary number. These studies, therefore, often develop a rubric or measure for valuing the species richness number(s) or adopt one from previous studies on similar ecosystems.
Recombination	In cosmology, recombination refers to the epoch at which charged electrons and protons first became bound to form electrically neutral hydrogen atoms. After the Big Bang, the universe was a hot, dense plasma of photons, electrons, and protons. This plasma was effectively opaque to electromagnetic radiation, as the distance each photon could travel before encountering a charged particle was very short.
Domestication	Domestication is the process whereby a population of animals or plants, through a process of selection, becomes accustomed to human provision and control. A defining characteristic of domestication is artificial selection by humans. Humans have brought these populations under their control and care for a wide range of reasons: to produce food or valuable commodities (such as wool, cotton, or silk), for help with various types of work (such as transportation, protection, and warfare), scientific research, or simply to enjoy as companions or ornaments.
Roundup	Roundup is the brand name of a systemic, broad-spectrum herbicide produced by the U.S. company Monsanto, and contains the active ingredient glyphosate. Glyphosate is the most widely used herbicide in the USA, and Roundup has been the number one selling herbicide worldwide since at least 1980.

Visit Cram101.com for full Practice Exams

5. Evolution of Biodiversity

CHAPTER HIGHLIGHTS & NOTES: KEY TERMS, PEOPLE, PLACES, CONCEPTS

	As of 2009, sales of Roundup herbicides represent about 10% of Monsanto's revenue due to competition from Chinese producers of other glyphosate-based herbicides; the overall Roundup line of products represents about half of Monsanto's yearly revenue.
	Monsanto developed and patented the glyphosate molecule in the 1970s, and marketed Roundup from 1973. It retained exclusive rights in the US until its US patent expired in September, 2000, and maintained a predominant marketshare in countries where the patent expired earlier.
Charles Darwin	Charles Darwin, FRS (12 February 1809 - 19 April 1882) was an English naturalist. He established that all species of life have descended over time from common ancestors, and proposed the scientific theory that this branching pattern of evolution resulted from a process that he called natural selection, in which the struggle for existence has a similar effect to the artificial selection involved in selective breeding.
	Charles Darwin published his theory of evolution with compelling evidence in his 1859 book On the Origin of Species, overcoming scientific rejection of earlier concepts of transmutation of species.
Allopatric speciation	Allopatric speciation is speciation that occurs when biological populations of the same species become isolated due to geographical changes such mountain building or social changes such emigration. The isolated populations then undergo genotypic and/or phenotypic divergence : (a) they become subjected to different selective pressures, (b) they independently undergo genetic drift, and (c) different mutations arise in the populations' gene pools.
	The separate populations over time may evolve distinctly different characteristics.
Sympatric speciation	Sympatric speciation is the proce through which new species evolve from a single ancestral species while inhabiting the same geographic region. In evolutionary biology and biogeography, sympatric and sympatry are terms referring to organisms whose ranges overlap or are even identical, so that they occur together at least in some places. If these organisms are closely related (e.g. sister species), such a distribution may be the result of sympatric speciation.
Extinction	In biology and ecology, extinction is the end of an organism or of a group of organisms (taxon), normally a species. The moment of extinction is generally considered to be the death of the last individual of the species, although the capacity to breed and recover may have been lost before this point. Because a species' potential range may be very large, determining this moment is difficult, and is usually done retrospectively.
Lake Tanganyika	Lake Tanganyika is an African Great Lake. It is estimated to be the second largest freshwater lake in the world by volume, and the second deepest, after Lake Baikal in Siberia; it is also the world's longest freshwater lake.

Visit Cram101.com for full Practice Exams

5. Evolution of Biodiversity

CHAPTER HIGHLIGHTS & NOTES: KEY TERMS, PEOPLE, PLACES, CONCEPTS

Genetically modified organism	A genetically modified organism or genetically engineered organism (GEO) is an organism whose genetic material has been altered using genetic engineering techniques. These techniques, generally known as recombinant DNA technology, use DNA molecules from different sources, which are combined into one molecule to create a new set of genes. This DNA is then transferred into an organism, giving it modified or novel genes.
Species distribution	Species distribution is the manner in which a biological taxon is spatially arranged. Species distribution is not to be confused with dispersal, which is the movement of individuals away from their area of origin or from centers of high population density. A similar concept is the species range.
Fossil	Fossils are the preserved remains or traces of animals (also known as zoolites), plants, and other organisms from the remote past. The totality of fossils, both discovered and undiscovered, and their placement in fossiliferous (fossil-containing) rock formations and sedimentary layers (strata) is known as the fossil record.
	The study of fossils across geological time, how they were formed, and the evolutionary relationships between taxa (phylogeny) are some of the most important functions of the science of paleontology.
Polar	The Global Geospace Science (GGS) Polar Satellite was a NASA science spacecraft designed to study the polar magnetosphere and aurora. It was launched into orbit in February 1996, and continued operations until the program was terminated in April 2008. The spacecraft remains in orbit, though it is now inactive. Polar is the sister ship to GGS Wind.
Biodiversity hotspot	A biodiversity hotspot is a biogeographic region with a significant reservoir of biodiversity that is under threat from humans.
	The concept of biodiversity hotspots was originated by Norman Myers in two articles in 'The Environmentalist' (1988), & 1990 revised after thorough analysis by Myers and others in 'Hotspots: Earth's Biologically Richest and Most Endangered Terrestrial Ecoregions'.
	To qualify as a biodiversity hotspot on Myers 2000 edition of the hotspot-map, a region must meet two strict criteria: it must contain at least 0.5% or 1,500 species of vascular plants as endemics, and it has to have lost at least 70% of its primary vegetation.

Visit Cram101.com for full Practice Exams

5. Evolution of Biodiversity

CHAPTER QUIZ: KEY TERMS, PEOPLE, PLACES, CONCEPTS

1. _____s are the preserved remains or traces of animals (also known as zoolites), plants, and other organisms from the remote past. The totality of _____s, both discovered and undiscovered, and their placement in fossiliferous (_____-containing) rock formations and sedimentary layers (strata) is known as the _____ record.

   The study of _____s across geological time, how they were formed, and the evolutionary relationships between taxa (phylogeny) are some of the most important functions of the science of paleontology.

   a. Fossil collecting
   b. Francevillian Group Fossil
   c. Fossil
   d. Glyptochiton

2. _____ is speciation that occurs when biological populations of the same species become isolated due to geographical changes such mountain building or social changes such emigration. The isolated populations then undergo genotypic and/or phenotypic divergence : (a) they become subjected to different selective pressures, (b) they independently undergo genetic drift, and (c) different mutations arise in the populations' gene pools.

   The separate populations over time may evolve distinctly different characteristics.

   a. Alternative stable state
   b. Allopatric speciation
   c. Association
   d. Autoecology

3. _____ is the brand name of a systemic, broad-spectrum herbicide produced by the U.S. company Monsanto, and contains the active ingredient glyphosate. Glyphosate is the most widely used herbicide in the USA, and _____ has been the number one selling herbicide worldwide since at least 1980. As of 2009, sales of _____ herbicides represent about 10% of Monsanto's revenue due to competition from Chinese producers of other glyphosate-based herbicides; the overall _____ line of products represents about half of Monsanto's yearly revenue.

   Monsanto developed and patented the glyphosate molecule in the 1970s, and marketed _____ from 1973. It retained exclusive rights in the US until its US patent expired in September, 2000, and maintained a predominant marketshare in countries where the patent expired earlier.

   a. Roundup
   b. Toxaphene
   c. Tributyltin
   d. Triclosan

4. . The Global Geospace Science (GGS) _____ Satellite was a NASA science spacecraft designed to study the _____ magnetosphere and aurora. It was launched into orbit in February 1996, and continued operations until the program was terminated in April 2008. The spacecraft remains in orbit, though it is now inactive. _____ is the sister ship to GGS Wind.

Visit Cram101.com for full Practice Exams

5. Evolution of Biodiversity

CHAPTER QUIZ: KEY TERMS, PEOPLE, PLACES, CONCEPTS

a. POLDER
b. Polymer Battery Experiment
c. PoSAT-1
d. Polar

5. _____ is the number of different species in a given area. It is represented in equation form as S.

_____ is the fundamental unit in which to assess the homogeneity of an environment. Typically, _____ is used in conservation studies to determine the sensitivity of ecosystems and their resident species. The actual number of species calculated alone is largely an arbitrary number. These studies, therefore, often develop a rubric or measure for valuing the _____ number(s) or adopt one from previous studies on similar ecosystems.

a. Juglone
b. Janzen-Connell hypothesis
c. Species richness
d. Base-richness

Visit Cram101.com for full Practice Exams

Visit Cram101.com for full Practice Exams

ANSWER KEY
5. Evolution of Biodiversity

1. c
2. b
3. a
4. d
5. c

You can take the complete Chapter Practice Test

for 5. Evolution of Biodiversity
on all key terms, persons, places, and concepts.

Online 99 Cents

http://www.epub89.16.23086.5.cram101.com/

Use www.Cram101.com for all your study needs

including Cram101's online interactive problem solving labs in

chemistry, statistics, mathematics, and more.

Visit Cram101.com for full Practice Exams

6. Population and Community Ecology

CHAPTER OUTLINE: KEY TERMS, PEOPLE, PLACES, CONCEPTS

Ecological succession

Secondary succession

Biosphere

Ecosystem

Population ecology

Population density

Population size

Carrying capacity

Protozoa

Sex ratio

Exponential growth

Competitive exclusion principle

Charles Darwin

Predation

Parasitoid

Commensalism

Keystone species

Keystone

Starfish

Primary succession

Island biogeography

Visit Cram101.com for full Practice Exams

6. Population and Community Ecology
CHAPTER OUTLINE: KEY TERMS, PEOPLE, PLACES, CONCEPTS

Species richness

CHAPTER HIGHLIGHTS & NOTES: KEY TERMS, PEOPLE, PLACES, CONCEPTS

Ecological succession	Ecological succession, is the phenomenon or process by which an ecological community undergoes more or less orderly and predictable changes following disturbance or initial colonization of new habitat. Succession was among the first theories advanced in ecology and the study of succession remains at the core of ecological science. Succession may be initiated either by formation of new, unoccupied habitat (e.g., a lava flow or a severe landslide) or by some form of disturbance (e.g. fire, severe windthrow, logging) of an existing community.
Secondary succession	Secondary succession is one of the two types of ecological succession of plant life. As opposed to the first, primary succession, secondary succession is a process started by an event (e.g. forest fire, harvesting, hurricane) that reduces an already established ecosystem (e.g. a forest or a wheat field) to a smaller population of species, and as such secondary succession occurs on preexisting soil whereas primary succession usually occurs in a place lacking soil.
Biosphere	The biosphere is the global sum of all ecosystems. It can also be called the zone of life on Earth, a closed (apart from solar and cosmic radiation), and self-regulating system. From the broadest biophysiological point of view, the biosphere is the global ecological system integrating all living beings and their relationships, including their interaction with the elements of the lithosphere, hydrosphere, and atmosphere.
Ecosystem	An ecosystem is a community of living organisms (plants, animals and microbes) in conjunction with the nonliving components of their environment (things like air, water and mineral soil), interacting as a system. These components are regarded as linked together through nutrient cycles and energy flows. As ecosystems are defined by the network of interactions among organisms, and between organisms and their environment, they can come in any size but usually encompass specific, limited spaces (although some scientists say that the entire planet is an ecosystem).
Population ecology	Population ecology is a major sub-field of ecology that deals with the dynamics of species populations and how these populations interact with the environment. It is the study of how the population sizes of species living together in groups change over time and space. The development of population ecology owes much to demography and actuarial life tables.
Population density	Population density is a measurement of population per unit area or unit volume.

Visit Cram101.com for full Practice Exams

6. Population and Community Ecology

CHAPTER HIGHLIGHTS & NOTES: KEY TERMS, PEOPLE, PLACES, CONCEPTS

It is frequently applied to living organisms, and particularly to humans. It is a key geographic term.

Population size

In population genetics and population ecology, population size is the number of individual organisms in a population.

The effective population size is defined as 'the number of breeding individuals in an idealized population that would show the same amount of dispersion of allele frequencies under random genetic drift or the same amount of inbreeding as the population under consideration.' N_e is usually less than N (the absolute population size) and this has important applications in conservation genetics.

Small population size results in increased genetic drift.

Carrying capacity

The carrying capacity of a biological species in an environment is the maximum population size of the species that the environment can sustain indefinitely, given the food, habitat, water and other necessities available in the environment. In population biology, carrying capacity is defined as the environment's maximal load, which is different from the concept of population equilibrium.

For the human population, more complex variables such as sanitation and medical care are sometimes considered as part of the necessary establishment.

Protozoa

Protozoa are a diverse group of unicellular eukaryotic organisms, many of which are motile. Originally, protozoa had been defined as unicellular protists with animal-like behavior, e.g., movement. Protozoa were regarded as the partner group of protists to protophyta, which have plant-like behaviour, e.g., photosynthesis.

Sex ratio

Sex ratio is the ratio of males to females in a population. The primary sex ratio is the ratio at the time of conception, secondary sex ratio is the ratio at time of birth, and tertiary sex ratio is the ratio of mature organisms.

The human sex ratio is of particular interest to anthropologists and demographers. In humans the secondary sex ratio is commonly assumed to be 105 boys to 100 girls (which sometimes is shortened to 'a ratio of 105'). In human societies, however, sex ratios at birth may be considerably skewed by natural reasons such as the age of mother at birth, and unnatural reasons such as sex-selective abortion. The CIA estimates that the current world wide sex ratio at birth is 107 boys to 100 girls. The value for the entire world population is 101 males to 100 females.

Exponential growth

Exponential growth occurs when the growth rate of the value of a mathematical function is proportional to the function's current value. Exponential decay occurs in the same way when the growth rate is negative. In the case of a discrete domain of definition with equal intervals it is also called geometric growth or geometric decay (the function values form a geometric progression).

Visit Cram101.com for full Practice Exams

6. Population and Community Ecology

CHAPTER HIGHLIGHTS & NOTES: KEY TERMS, PEOPLE, PLACES, CONCEPTS

Competitive exclusion principle	In ecology, the competitive exclusion principle, is a proposition which states that two species competing for the same resources cannot coexist if other ecological factors are constant. When one species has even the slightest advantage or edge over another, then the one with the advantage will dominate in the long term. One of the two competitors will always overcome the other, leading to either the extinction of this competitor or an evolutionary or behavioral shift towards a different ecological niche.
Charles Darwin	Charles Darwin, FRS (12 February 1809 - 19 April 1882) was an English naturalist. He established that all species of life have descended over time from common ancestors, and proposed the scientific theory that this branching pattern of evolution resulted from a process that he called natural selection, in which the struggle for existence has a similar effect to the artificial selection involved in selective breeding. Charles Darwin published his theory of evolution with compelling evidence in his 1859 book On the Origin of Species, overcoming scientific rejection of earlier concepts of transmutation of species.
Predation	In ecology, predation describes a biological interaction where a predator (an organism that is hunting) feeds on its prey (the organism that is attacked). Predators may or may not kill their prey prior to feeding on them, but the act of predation always results in the death of its prey and the eventual absorption of the prey's tissue through consumption. Other categories of consumption are herbivory (eating parts of plants) and detritivory, the consumption of dead organic material (detritus).
Parasitoid	A parasitoid is an organism that spends a significant portion of its life history attached to or within a single host organism in a relationship that is in essence parasitic; unlike a true parasite, however, it ultimately sterilises or kills, and sometimes consumes, the host. Thus parasitoids are similar to typical parasites except in the more dire prognosis for the host. The term parasitoid was coined in 1913 by the German writer O. M. Reuter to describe the strategy in which, during its development, the parasite lives in or on the body of a single host individual, eventually killing that host, the adult parasitoid being free-living.
Commensalism	In ecology, commensalism is a class of relationship between two organisms where one organism benefits but the other is neutral (there is no harm or benefit). There are two other types of association: mutualism (where both organisms benefit) and parasitism (one organism benefits and the other one is harmed). Originally, the term was used to describe the use of waste food by second animals, like the carcass eaters that follow hunting animals, but wait until they have finished their meal.
Keystone species	A keystone species is a species that has a disproportionately large effect on its environment relative to its abundance.

Visit Cram101.com for full Practice Exams

6. Population and Community Ecology

CHAPTER HIGHLIGHTS & NOTES: KEY TERMS, PEOPLE, PLACES, CONCEPTS

Such species play a critical role in maintaining the structure of an ecological community, affecting many other organisms in an ecosystem and helping to determine the types and numbers of various other species in the community.

The role that a keystone species plays in its ecosystem is analogous to the role of a keystone in an arch.

Keystone

Keystone refers to a type of limestone, or coral rag, quarried in the Florida Keys, in particular from Windley Key fossil quarry, which is now a State Park of Florida. The limestone is Pleistocene in age, and the rock primarily consists of scleractinian coral, such as Elkhorn coral and Brain coral.

The Hurricane Monument, commemorating victims of the Labor Day Hurricane of 1935, and located at mile marker 82 on US Route 1 near Islamorada, is constructed of keystone, as is the David W. Dyer Federal Building and United States Courthouse.

Starfish

Starfish are echinoderms belonging to the class Asteroidea. The names 'starfish' and 'sea star' essentially refer to members of the class Asteroidea. However, common usage frequently finds these names also applied to ophiuroids, which are correctly referred to as 'brittle stars' or 'basket stars'.

Primary succession

Primary succession is one of two types of biological and ecological succession of plant life, occurring in an environment in which new substrate devoid of vegetation and usually lacking soil, such as a lava flow or area left from retreated glacier, is deposited. In other words, it is the gradual growth of an ecosystem over a longer period of time.

In contrast, secondary succession occurs on substrate that previously supported vegetation before an ecological disturbance such as forest fire, tsunami, flood, destroyed the plant life.

Island biogeography

Island biogeography is a field within biogeography that attempts to establish and explain the factors that affect the species richness of natural communities. The theory was developed to explain species richness of actual islands. It has since been extended to mountains surrounded by deserts, lakes surrounded by dry land, fragmented forest and even natural habitats surrounded by human-altered landscapes.

Species richness

Species richness is the number of different species in a given area. It is represented in equation form as S.

Species richness is the fundamental unit in which to assess the homogeneity of an environment. Typically, species richness is used in conservation studies to determine the sensitivity of ecosystems and their resident species. The actual number of species calculated alone is largely an arbitrary number.

Visit Cram101.com for full Practice Exams

6. Population and Community Ecology

CHAPTER QUIZ: KEY TERMS, PEOPLE, PLACES, CONCEPTS

1. _____, FRS (12 February 1809 - 19 April 1882) was an English naturalist. He established that all species of life have descended over time from common ancestors, and proposed the scientific theory that this branching pattern of evolution resulted from a process that he called natural selection, in which the struggle for existence has a similar effect to the artificial selection involved in selective breeding.

   _____ published his theory of evolution with compelling evidence in his 1859 book On the Origin of Species, overcoming scientific rejection of earlier concepts of transmutation of species.

   a. Charles Darwin
   b. Sinibaldo I Ordelaffi
   c. Rowland Hill
   d. Rank-size distribution

2. _____ is one of the two types of ecological succession of plant life. As opposed to the first, primary succession, _____ is a process started by an event (e.g. forest fire, harvesting, hurricane) that reduces an already established ecosystem (e.g. a forest or a wheat field) to a smaller population of species, and as such _____ occurs on preexisting soil whereas primary succession usually occurs in a place lacking soil.

   a. Natural environment
   b. Juglone
   c. Secondary succession
   d. Krakatoa

3. _____ is the number of different species in a given area. It is represented in equation form as S.

   _____ is the fundamental unit in which to assess the homogeneity of an environment. Typically, _____ is used in conservation studies to determine the sensitivity of ecosystems and their resident species. The actual number of species calculated alone is largely an arbitrary number. These studies, therefore, often develop a rubric or measure for valuing the _____ number(s) or adopt one from previous studies on similar ecosystems.

   a. Species richness
   b. Gibbons v. Ogden
   c. Krakatoa
   d. Trackway

4. . In ecology, _____ describes a biological interaction where a predator (an organism that is hunting) feeds on its prey (the organism that is attacked). Predators may or may not kill their prey prior to feeding on them, but the act of _____ always results in the death of its prey and the eventual absorption of the prey's tissue through consumption. Other categories of consumption are herbivory (eating parts of plants) and detritivory, the consumption of dead organic material (detritus).

   a. Pyrethrin
   b. Pyrethrum
   c. Predation

Visit Cram101.com for full Practice Exams

6. Population and Community Ecology

CHAPTER QUIZ: KEY TERMS, PEOPLE, PLACES, CONCEPTS

5. _____, is the phenomenon or process by which an ecological community undergoes more or less orderly and predictable changes following disturbance or initial colonization of new habitat. Succession was among the first theories advanced in ecology and the study of succession remains at the core of ecological science. Succession may be initiated either by formation of new, unoccupied habitat (e.g., a lava flow or a severe landslide) or by some form of disturbance (e.g. fire, severe windthrow, logging) of an existing community.

a. Ecological succession
b. Endangered Species Act
c. United Nations Framework Convention on Climate Change
d. Absent-minded professor

Visit Cram101.com for full Practice Exams

ANSWER KEY
6. Population and Community Ecology

1. a
2. c
3. a
4. c
5. a

You can take the complete Chapter Practice Test

for 6. Population and Community Ecology
on all key terms, persons, places, and concepts.

Online 99 Cents

http://www.epub89.16.23086.6.cram101.com/

Use www.Cram101.com for all your study needs

including Cram101's online interactive problem solving labs in

chemistry, statistics, mathematics, and more.

Visit Cram101.com for full Practice Exams

7. The Human Population

CHAPTER OUTLINE: KEY TERMS, PEOPLE, PLACES, CONCEPTS

	Demography
	Birth rate
	Doubling time
	Total fertility rate
	Infant mortality
	Population pyramid
	Population momentum
	Population growth
	Demographic transition
	Population size
	Sustainable development
	Millennium Ecosystem Assessment

CHAPTER HIGHLIGHTS & NOTES: KEY TERMS, PEOPLE, PLACES, CONCEPTS

Demography

Demography is the statistical study of human populations and sub-populations. It can be a very general science that can be applied to any kind of dynamic human population, that is, one that changes over time or space . It encompasses the study of the size, structure, and distribution of these populations, and spatial and/or temporal changes in them in response to birth, migration, aging and death.

Birth rate

The birth rate is typically the rate of births in a population over time. The rate of births in a population is calculated in several ways: live births from a universal registration system for births, deaths, and marriages; population counts from a census, and estimation through specialized demographic techniques. The birth rate are used to calculate population growth.

Visit Cram101.com for full Practice Exams

7. The Human Population

CHAPTER HIGHLIGHTS & NOTES: KEY TERMS, PEOPLE, PLACES, CONCEPTS

Doubling time	The doubling time is the period of time required for a quantity to double in size or value. It is applied to population growth, inflation, resource extraction, consumption of goods, compound interest, the volume of malignant tumours, and many other things which tend to grow over time. When the relative growth rate (not the absolute growth rate) is constant, the quantity undergoes exponential growth and has a constant doubling time or period which can be calculated directly from the growth rate.
Total fertility rate	The total fertility rate of a population is the average number of children that would be born to a woman over her lifetime if (1) she were to experience the exact current age-specific fertility rates (ASFRs) through her lifetime, and (2) she were to survive from birth through the end of her reproductive life. It is obtained by summing the single-year age-specific rates at a given time.
Infant mortality	Infant mortality is defined as the number of infant deaths (one year of age or younger) per 1000 live births. Traditionally, the most common cause worldwide was dehydration from diarrhea. However, the spreading information about Oral Re-hydration Solution (a mixture of salts, sugar, and water) to mothers around the world has decreased the rate of children dying from dehydration.
Population pyramid	A population pyramid, is a graphical illustration that shows the distribution of various age groups in a human population (typically that of a country or region of the world), which ideally forms the shape of a pyramid when the region is healthy. It is also used in Ecology to determine the overall age distribution of a population; an indication of the reproductive capabilities and likelihood of the continuation of a species. It typically consists of two back-to-back bar graphs, with the population plotted on the X-axis and age on the Y-axis, one showing the number of males and one showing females in a particular population in five-year age groups (also called cohorts).
Population momentum	Population momentum refers to population growth at the national level which would occur even if levels of childbearing immediately declined to replacement level. For countries with above-replacement fertility (greater than 2.1 children per woman), population momentum represents natural increase to the population. For below-replacement countries, momentum corresponds to a population decline.
Population growth	Population growth is the change in a population over time, and can be quantified as the change in the number of individuals of any species in a population using 'per unit time' for measurement. Population growth is determined by four factors, births (B), deaths (D), immigrants (I), and emigrants (E). Using a formula expressed as $\Delta P \equiv (B-D)+(I-E)$

Visit Cram101.com for full Practice Exams

7. The Human Population

CHAPTER HIGHLIGHTS & NOTES: KEY TERMS, PEOPLE, PLACES, CONCEPTS

	In other words, the population growth of a period can be calculated in two parts, natural growth of population (B-D) and mechanical growth of population (I-E), in which mechanical growth of population is mainly affected by social factors, e.g. the advanced economies are growing faster while the backward economies are growing slowly even with negative growth.
Demographic transition	The demographic transition is the transition from high birth and death rates to low birth and death rates as a country develops from a pre-industrial to an industrialized economic system. The theory is based on an interpretation of demographic history developed in 1929 by the American demographer Warren Thompson (1887-1973). Thompson observed changes, or transitions, in birth and death rates in industrialized societies over the previous 200 years.
Population size	In population genetics and population ecology, population size is the number of individual organisms in a population. The effective population size is defined as 'the number of breeding individuals in an idealized population that would show the same amount of dispersion of allele frequencies under random genetic drift or the same amount of inbreeding as the population under consideration.' N_e is usually less than N (the absolute population size) and this has important applications in conservation genetics. Small population size results in increased genetic drift.
Sustainable development	Sustainable development is a pattern of growth in which resource use aims to meet human needs while preserving the environment so that these needs can be met not only in the present, but also for generations to come (sometimes taught as ELF-Environment, Local people, Future). The term sustainable development was used by the Brundtland Commission which coined what has become the most often-quoted definition of sustainable development as development that 'meets the needs of the present without compromising the ability of future generations to meet their own needs.' Sustainable development ties together concern for the carrying capacity of natural systems with the social challenges facing humanity. As early as the 1970s 'sustainability' was employed to describe an economy 'in equilibrium with basic ecological support systems.' Ecologists have pointed to The Limits to Growth, and presented the alternative of a 'steady state economy' in order to address environmental concerns.
Millennium Ecosystem Assessment	The Millennium Ecosystem Assessment, released in 2005, is an international synthesis by over 1000 of the world's leading biological scientists that analyzes the state of the Earth's ecosystems and provides summaries and guidelines for decision-makers. It concludes that human activity is having a significant and escalating impact on the biodiversity of world ecosystems, reducing both their resilience and biocapacity.

Visit Cram101.com for full Practice Exams

7. The Human Population

CHAPTER QUIZ: KEY TERMS, PEOPLE, PLACES, CONCEPTS

1. The _____ is the period of time required for a quantity to double in size or value. It is applied to population growth, inflation, resource extraction, consumption of goods, compound interest, the volume of malignant tumours, and many other things which tend to grow over time. When the relative growth rate (not the absolute growth rate) is constant, the quantity undergoes exponential growth and has a constant _____ or period which can be calculated directly from the growth rate.

   a. growth curve
   b. Doubling time
   c. Gibbons v. Ogden
   d. Natural resource management

2. _____ is defined as the number of infant deaths (one year of age or younger) per 1000 live births. Traditionally, the most common cause worldwide was dehydration from diarrhea. However, the spreading information about Oral Re-hydration Solution (a mixture of salts, sugar, and water) to mothers around the world has decreased the rate of children dying from dehydration.

   a. Odyssey
   b. Endangered Species Act
   c. United Nations Framework Convention on Climate Change
   d. Infant mortality

3. The _____ is typically the rate of births in a population over time. The rate of births in a population is calculated in several ways: live births from a universal registration system for births, deaths, and marriages; population counts from a census, and estimation through specialized demographic techniques. The _____ are used to calculate population growth.

   a. Birth rate
   b. Human ecology
   c. Human geography
   d. Natural resource management

4. _____ is the statistical study of human populations and sub-populations. It can be a very general science that can be applied to any kind of dynamic human population, that is, one that changes over time or space . It encompasses the study of the size, structure, and distribution of these populations, and spatial and/or temporal changes in them in response to birth, migration, aging and death.

   a. Healthy city
   b. Demography
   c. Human geography
   d. Natural resource management

5. . The _____ of a population is the average number of children that would be born to a woman over her lifetime if (1) she were to experience the exact current age-specific fertility rates (ASFRs) through her lifetime, and (2) she were to survive from birth through the end of her reproductive life. It is obtained by summing the single-year age-specific rates at a given time.

Visit Cram101.com for full Practice Exams

7. The Human Population

CHAPTER QUIZ: KEY TERMS, PEOPLE, PLACES, CONCEPTS

a. reproduction

b. Total fertility rate

c. Gibbons v. Ogden

d. Natural resource management

Visit Cram101.com for full Practice Exams

ANSWER KEY
7. The Human Population

1. b
2. d
3. a
4. b
5. b

You can take the complete Chapter Practice Test

for 7. The Human Population
on all key terms, persons, places, and concepts.

Online 99 Cents

http://www.epub89.16.23086.7.cram101.com/

Use www.Cram101.com for all your study needs

including Cram101's online interactive problem solving labs in

chemistry, statistics, mathematics, and more.

Visit Cram101.com for full Practice Exams

8. Earth Systems

CHAPTER OUTLINE: KEY TERMS, PEOPLE, PLACES, CONCEPTS

Formation

Asthenosphere

Convection

Hotspot

Lithosphere

Magma

Pangaea

Plate tectonics

Seafloor spreading

Subduction

Geologic time scale

Hawaiian Islands

Divergent boundary

Earthquake

Himalayas

Rock cycle

Global warming

Basalt

Igneous rock

Metamorphic rock

Obsidian

Visit Cram101.com for full Practice Exams

8. Earth Systems
CHAPTER OUTLINE: KEY TERMS, PEOPLE, PLACES, CONCEPTS

Sedimentary rock

Sandstone

Feldspar

Deposition

Erosion

Parent material

Soil evolution

Subsoil

Topsoil

Soil texture

Permeability

Cation exchange capacity

Cation

Degradation

Bauxite

Placer mining

Surface mining

Visit Cram101.com for full Practice Exams

8. Earth Systems

CHAPTER HIGHLIGHTS & NOTES: KEY TERMS, PEOPLE, PLACES, CONCEPTS

Formation	A formation is the fundamental unit of lithostratigraphy. A formation consists of a certain number of rock strata that have a comparable lithology, facies or other similar properties. Formations are not defined on the thickness of the rock strata they consist of and the thickness of different formations can therefore vary widely.
Asthenosphere	The asthenosphere is the highly viscous mechanically weak ductilely-deforming region of the upper mantle of the Earth. It lies below the lithosphere, at depths between 100 and 200 km (~ 62 and 124 miles) below the surface, but perhaps extending as deep as 700 km (~ 435 miles). Characteristics The asthenosphere is a portion of the upper mantle just below the lithosphere that is involved in plate tectonic movements and isostatic adjustments.
Convection	Convection is the concerted, collective movement of ensembles of molecules within fluids (i.e. liquids, gases) and rheids. Convection of mass cannot take place in solids, since neither bulk current flows nor significant diffusion can take place in solids. Diffusion of heat can take place in solids, but is referred to separately in that case as heat conduction.
Hotspot	The places known as hotspots or hot spots in geology are volcanic regions thought to be fed by underlying mantle that is anomalously hot compared with the mantle elsewhere. They may be unanimously hot, and provide a great deal of molten magma. They may be on, near to, or far from tectonic plate boundaries.
Lithosphere	The lithosphere is the rigid outermost shell of a rocky planet. On Earth, it comprises the crust and the portion of the upper mantle that behaves elastically on time scales of thousands of years or greater. Earth's lithosphere In the Earth, the lithosphere includes the crust and the uppermost mantle, which constitute the hard and rigid outer layer of the Earth.
Magma	Magma is a mixture of molten or semi molten rock, volatiles and solids that is found beneath the surface of the Earth, and is expected to exist on other terrestrial planets. Besides molten rock, magma may also contain suspended crystals and dissolved gas and sometimes also gas bubbles. Magma often collects in magma chambers that may feed a volcano or turn into a pluton.
Pangaea	Pangaea was the supercontinent that existed during the Paleozoic and Mesozoic eras about 250 million years ago, before the component continents were separated into their current configuration. The name was coined during a 1926 symposium discussing Alfred Wegener's theory of continental drift.

Visit Cram101.com for full Practice Exams

8. Earth Systems

CHAPTER HIGHLIGHTS & NOTES: KEY TERMS, PEOPLE, PLACES, CONCEPTS

Plate tectonics

Plate tectonics is a scientific theory which describes the large scale motions of Earth's lithosphere. The theory builds on the older concepts of continental drift, developed during the first decades of the 20th century (one of the most famous advocates was Alfred Wegener), and was accepted by the majority of the geoscientific community when the concepts of seafloor spreading were developed in the late 1950s and early 1960s. The lithosphere is broken up into what are called tectonic plates.

Seafloor spreading

Seafloor spreading is a process that occurs at mid-ocean ridges, where new oceanic crust is formed through volcanic activity and then gradually moves away from the ridge. Seafloor spreading helps explain continental drift in the theory of plate tectonics.

Earlier theories (e.g., by Alfred Wegener and Alexander du Toit) of continental drift were that continents 'plowed' through the sea.

Subduction

In geology, subduction is the process that takes place at convergent boundaries by which one tectonic plate moves under another tectonic plate, sinking into the Earth's mantle, as the plates converge. These 3D regions of mantle downwellings are known as 'Subduction Zones'. A subduction zone is an area on Earth where two tectonic plates move towards one another and one slides under the other.

Geologic time scale

The geologic time scale is a system of chronological measurement that relates stratigraphy to time, and is used by geologists, paleontologists, and other earth scientists to describe the timing and relationships between events that have occurred throughout Earth's history. The table of geologic time spans presented here agrees with the dates and nomenclature set forth by the International Commission on Stratigraphy standard color codes of the International Commission on Stratigraphy.

Evidence from radiometric dating indicates that the Earth is about 4.54 billion years old.

Hawaiian Islands

The Hawaiian Islands are an archipelago of eight major islands, several atolls, numerous smaller islets, and undersea seamounts in the North Pacific Ocean, extending some 1,500 miles (2,400 kilometres) from the island of Hawaii in the south to northernmost Kure Atoll. Once known as the 'Sandwich Islands', the name chosen by James Cook in honour of the then First Lord of the Admiralty John Montagu, 4th Earl of Sandwich, the archipelago now takes its name from the largest island in the cluster. The U.S. state of Hawaii occupies the archipelago almost in its entirety, with the sole exception of Midway island, which is instead an unincorporated territory within the United States Minor Outlying Islands.

Divergent boundary

In plate tectonics, a divergent boundary is a linear feature that exists between two tectonic plates that are moving away from each other. Divergent boundaries within continents initially produce rifts which produce rift valleys. Most active divergent plate boundaries occur between oceanic plates and exist as mid-oceanic ridges.

Visit Cram101.com for full Practice Exams

8. Earth Systems

CHAPTER HIGHLIGHTS & NOTES: KEY TERMS, PEOPLE, PLACES, CONCEPTS

Earthquake	An earthquake is the result of a sudden release of energy in the Earth's crust that creates seismic waves. The seismicity or seismic activity of an area refers to the frequency, type and size of earthquakes experienced over a period of time. Earthquakes are measured using observations from seismometers.
Himalayas	The Himalayas, is a mountain range immediately at the north of the Indian subcontinent. By extension, it is also the name of a massive mountain system that includes the Karakoram, the Hindu Kush, and other, lesser, ranges that extend out from the Pamir Knot. Together, the Himalayan mountain system is the world's highest, and home to the world's highest peaks, the Eight-thousanders, which include Mount Everest and K2. To comprehend the enormous scale of this mountain range, consider that Aconcagua, in the Andes, at 6,962 metres (22,841 ft) is the highest peak outside Asia, whereas the Himalayan system includes over 100 mountains exceeding 7,200 m (23,600 ft).
Rock cycle	The rock cycle is a fundamental concept in geology that describes the dynamic transitions through geologic time among the three main rock types: sedimentary, metamorphic, and igneous. As the diagram to the right illustrates, each type of rock is altered or destroyed when it is forced out of its equilibrium conditions. An igneous rock such as basalt may break down and dissolve when exposed to the atmosphere, or melt as it is subducted under a continent.
Global warming	Global warming refers to the rising average temperature of Earth's atmosphere and oceans, which began to increase in the late 19th century and is projected to continue rising. Since the early 20th century, Earth's average surface temperature has increased by about 0.8 °C (1.4 °F), with about two thirds of the increase occurring since 1980. Warming of the climate system is unequivocal, and scientists are more than 90% certain that most of it is caused by increasing concentrations of greenhouse gases produced by human activities such as deforestation and the burning of fossil fuels. These findings are recognized by the national science academies of all major industrialized nations.[A] Climate model projections are summarized in the 2007 Fourth Assessment Report (AR4) by the Intergovernmental Panel on Climate Change (IPCC).
Basalt	Basalt is a common extrusive igneous (volcanic) rock formed from the rapid cooling of basaltic lava exposed at or very near the surface of a planet or moon. By definition, basalt is an aphanitic igneous rock with less than 20% quartz and less than 10% feldspathoid by volume, and where at least 65% of the feldspar is in the form of plagioclase. (In comparison, granite has more than 20% quartz by volume).
Igneous rock	Igneous rock is one of the three main rock types, the others being sedimentary and metamorphic rock. Igneous rock is formed through the cooling and solidification of magma or lava.

Visit Cram101.com for full Practice Exams

8. Earth Systems

CHAPTER HIGHLIGHTS & NOTES: KEY TERMS, PEOPLE, PLACES, CONCEPTS

Metamorphic rock	Metamorphic rocks arise from the transformation of existing rock types, in a process called metamorphism, which means 'change in form'. The original rock (protolith) is subjected to heat (temperatures greater than 150 to 200 °C) and pressure (1500 bars), causing profound physical and/or chemical change. The protolith may be sedimentary rock, igneous rock or another older metamorphic rock.
Obsidian	Obsidian is a naturally occurring volcanic glass formed as an extrusive igneous rock. It is produced when felsic lava extruded from a volcano cools rapidly with minimum crystal growth. Obsidian is commonly found within the margins of rhyolitic lava flows known as obsidian flows, where the chemical composition (high silica content) induces a high viscosity and polymerization degree of the lava.
Sedimentary rock	Sedimentary rocks are types of rock that are formed by the deposition of material at the Earth's surface and within bodies of water. Sedimentation is the collective name for processes that cause mineral and/or organic particles (detritus) to settle and accumulate or minerals to precipitate from a solution. Particles that form a sedimentary rock by accumulating are called sediment.
Sandstone	Sandstone is a clastic sedimentary rock composed mainly of sand-sized minerals or rock grains. Most sandstone is composed of quartz and/or feldspar because these are the most common minerals in the Earth's crust. Like sand, sandstone may be any colour, but the most common colours are tan, brown, yellow, red, gray, pink, white and black.
Feldspar	Feldspars ($KAlSi_3O_8$ - $NaAlSi_3O_8$ - $CaAl_2Si_2O_8$) are a group of rock-forming tectosilicate minerals which make up as much as 60% of the Earth's crust. Feldspars crystallize from magma in both intrusive and extrusive igneous rocks, as veins, and are also present in many types of metamorphic rock. Feldspars are also found in many types of sedimentary rock.
Deposition	Deposition is a process in which gas transforms into solid (also known as desublimation). The reverse of deposition is sublimation. One example of deposition is the process by which, in sub-freezing air, water vapor changes directly to ice without first becoming a liquid.
Erosion	Erosion is the process by which soil and rock are removed from the Earth's surface by exogenetic processes such as wind or water flow, and then transported and deposited in other locations. While erosion is a natural process, human activities have increased by 10-40 times the rate at which erosion is occurring globally.

Visit Cram101.com for full Practice Exams

8. Earth Systems

CHAPTER HIGHLIGHTS & NOTES: KEY TERMS, PEOPLE, PLACES, CONCEPTS

Parent material	In soil science, parent material is the underlying geological material (generally bedrock or a superficial or drift deposit) in which soil horizons form. Soils typically inherit a great deal of structure and minerals from their parent material, and, as such, are often classified based upon their contents of consolidated or unconsolidated mineral material that has undergone some degree of physical or chemical weathering and the mode by which the materials were most recently transported.

Consolidated

Parent materials that are predominately composed of consolidated rock are termed residual parent material. |
| Soil evolution | Pedogenesis is the science and study of the processes that lead to the formation of soil (soil evolution) and first explored by the Russian geologist Vasily Dokuchaev (1846 - 1903), the so-called grandfather of soil science, who determined that soil formed over time as a consequence of climatic, mineral and biological processes which he demonstrated using the soil forming equation:Soil = f(C, PM, O) x time (where C = climate, PM = parent material, O = biological processes)

In 1941 the Swiss scientist Hans Jenny expanded Vasily Dokuchaev equation by adding relief/topology as a factor and separating the biological processes into the fauna and flora coming up with the equation:Soil = f(C, PM, R, O, V,) x time (where C = climate, PM = parent material, R = relief/topology, O = fauna, V = flora)

Pedogenesis is though more a parent than a branch of pedology, whose other aspects include the soil morphology, classification (taxonomy) of soils, and their distribution in nature, present and past (soil geography and paleopedology).

Climate regulates soil formation. Soils are more developed in areas with higher rainfall and more warmth. |
| Subsoil | Subsoil is the layer of soil under the topsoil on the surface of the ground. Like topsoil it is composed of a variable mixture of small particles such as sand, silt and/or clay, but it lacks the organic matter and humus content of topsoil. Below the subsoil is the substratum, which can be residual bedrock, sediments, or aeolian deposits. |
| Topsoil | Topsoil is the upper, outermost layer of soil, usually the top 2 inches (5.1 cm) to 8 inches (20 cm). It has the highest concentration of organic matter and microorganisms and is where most of the Earth's biological soil activity occurs.

Importance |

Visit Cram101.com for full Practice Exams

8. Earth Systems

CHAPTER HIGHLIGHTS & NOTES: KEY TERMS, PEOPLE, PLACES, CONCEPTS

Soil texture	Soil texture is a qualitative classification tool used in both the field and laboratory to determine classes for agricultural soils based on their physical texture. The classes are distinguished in the field by the 'textural feel' which can be further clarified by separating the relative proportions of sand, silt and clay using grading sieves: The Particle Size Distribution (PSD). The class is then used to determine crop suitability and to approximate the soils responses to environmental and management conditions such as drought or calcium (lime) requirements.
Permeability	Permeability is a property of foundry sand with respect to how well the sand can vent, i.e. how well gases pass through the sand.And in other words, permeability is the property by which we can know the ability of material to transmit fluid/gases. The permeability is commonly tested to see if it is correct for the casting conditions.
	The grain size, shape and distribution of the foundry sand, the type and quantity of bonding materials, the density to which the sand is rammed, and the percentage of moisture used for tempering the sand are important factors in regulating the degree of permeability.
Cation exchange capacity	In soil science, cation exchange capacity is the capacity of a soil for ion exchange of cations between the soil and the soil solution. Cation exchange capacity is used as a measure of fertility, nutrient retention capacity, and the capacity to protect groundwater from cation contamination. The Base Cation Saturation Ratio (BCSR) is a method of interpreting soil test results that is widely used in sustainable agriculture, supported by the National Sustainable Agriculture Information Service (ATTRA) and claimed to be successfully in use on over a million acres of farmland worldwide.
Cation	An ion is an atom or molecule in which the total number of electrons is not equal to the total number of protons, giving the atom a net positive or negative electrical charge.
	Ions can be created by both chemical and physical means. In chemical terms, if a neutral atom loses one or more electrons, it has a net positive charge and is known as a cation.
Degradation	In geology, degradation refers to the lowering of a fluvial surface, such as a stream bed or floodplain, through erosional processes. It is the opposite of aggradation. Degradation is characteristic of channel networks in which either bedrock erosion is taking place, or in systems that are sediment-starved and are therefore entraining more material than is being deposited.
Bauxite	Bauxite is an aluminium ore and is the main source of aluminium. This form of rock consists mostly of the minerals gibbsite $Al(OH)_3$, boehmite γ-AlO(OH), and diaspore α-AlO(OH), in a mixture with the two iron oxides goethite and hematite, the clay mineral kaolinite, and small amounts of anatase TiO_2. he village Les Baux in southern France, where it was first recognised as containing aluminium and named by the French geologist Pierre Berthier in 1821.
Placer mining	Placer mining is the mining of alluvial deposits for minerals.

Visit Cram101.com for full Practice Exams

8. Earth Systems

CHAPTER HIGHLIGHTS & NOTES: KEY TERMS, PEOPLE, PLACES, CONCEPTS

	This may be done by open-pit (also called open-cast mining) or by various surface excavating equipment or tunneling equipment.' It refers to mining the precious metal deposits (particularly gold and gemstones) found in alluvial deposits--deposits of sand and gravel in modern or ancient stream beds. The metal or gemstones, having been moved by stream flow from an original source such as a vein, is typically only a minuscule portion of the total deposit.
Surface mining	Surface mining is a type of mining in which soil and rock overlying the mineral deposit (the overburden) are removed. It is the opposite of underground mining, in which the overlying rock is left in place, and the mineral removed through shafts or tunnels.
	Surface mining began in the mid-sixteenth century and is practiced throughout the world, although the majority of surface mining occurs in North America. It gained popularity throughout the 20th century, and is now the predominant form of mining in coal beds such as those in Appalachia and America's Midwest.

CHAPTER QUIZ: KEY TERMS, PEOPLE, PLACES, CONCEPTS

1. _____ is the process by which soil and rock are removed from the Earth's surface by exogenetic processes such as wind or water flow, and then transported and deposited in other locations.

   While _____ is a natural process, human activities have increased by 10-40 times the rate at which _____ is occurring globally. Excessive _____ causes problems such as desertification, decreases in agricultural productivity due to land degradation, sedimentation of waterways, and ecological collapse due to loss of the nutrient rich upper soil layers.

   a. Evapotranspiration
   b. Erosion
   c. Institut National de la Recherche Agronomique
   d. Integrated pest management

2. . _____ refers to the rising average temperature of Earth's atmosphere and oceans, which began to increase in the late 19th century and is projected to continue rising. Since the early 20th century, Earth's average surface temperature has increased by about 0.8 °C (1.4 °F), with about two thirds of the increase occurring since 1980. Warming of the climate system is unequivocal, and scientists are more than 90% certain that most of it is caused by increasing concentrations of greenhouse gases produced by human activities such as deforestation and the burning of fossil fuels. These findings are recognized by the national science academies of all major industrialized nations.[A]

   Climate model projections are summarized in the 2007 Fourth Assessment Report (AR4) by the Intergovernmental Panel on Climate Change (IPCC).

Visit Cram101.com for full Practice Exams

8. Earth Systems

CHAPTER QUIZ: KEY TERMS, PEOPLE, PLACES, CONCEPTS

    a. Carbon budget
    b. Global warming
    c. Carbon dioxide flooding
    d. Carbon lock-in

3. A _____ is the fundamental unit of lithostratigraphy. A _____ consists of a certain number of rock strata that have a comparable lithology, facies or other similar properties. _____s are not defined on the thickness of the rock strata they consist of and the thickness of different _____s can therefore vary widely.

    a. Formation
    b. Wenatchee Dome
    c. Juglone
    d. Gibbons v. Ogden

4. _____ is a common extrusive igneous (volcanic) rock formed from the rapid cooling of basaltic lava exposed at or very near the surface of a planet or moon. By definition, _____ is an aphanitic igneous rock with less than 20% quartz and less than 10% feldspathoid by volume, and where at least 65% of the feldspar is in the form of plagioclase. (In comparison, granite has more than 20% quartz by volume).

    a. Basalt fiber
    b. Flood basalt
    c. Basalt
    d. Mugearite

5. _____ is a property of foundry sand with respect to how well the sand can vent, i.e. how well gases pass through the sand.And in other words, _____ is the property by which we can know the ability of material to transmit fluid/gases. The _____ is commonly tested to see if it is correct for the casting conditions.

The grain size, shape and distribution of the foundry sand, the type and quantity of bonding materials, the density to which the sand is rammed, and the percentage of moisture used for tempering the sand are important factors in regulating the degree of _____.

    a. Phase diagram
    b. Permeability
    c. Pseudo palladium
    d. Pyrometallurgy

Visit Cram101.com for full Practice Exams

Visit Cram101.com for full Practice Exams

ANSWER KEY
8. Earth Systems

1. b
2. b
3. a
4. c
5. b

You can take the complete Chapter Practice Test

for 8. Earth Systems
on all key terms, persons, places, and concepts.

Online 99 Cents

http://www.epub89.16.23086.8.cram101.com/

Use www.Cram101.com for all your study needs

including Cram101's online interactive problem solving labs in

chemistry, statistics, mathematics, and more.

Visit Cram101.com for full Practice Exams

9. Water Resources

CHAPTER OUTLINE: KEY TERMS, PEOPLE, PLACES, CONCEPTS

Fishery

Aquifer

Groundwater

Groundwater recharge

Water table

Saltwater intrusion

Floodplain

Dust Bowl

Drought

Fish ladder

Three Gorges Dam

Aqueduct

Colorado River Aqueduct

Desalination

Distillation

Reverse osmosis

Drip irrigation

Conservation

Water right

Visit Cram101.com for full Practice Exams

9. Water Resources

CHAPTER HIGHLIGHTS & NOTES: KEY TERMS, PEOPLE, PLACES, CONCEPTS

Fishery	Generally, a fishery is an entity engaged in raising or harvesting fish which is determined by some authority to be a fishery. According to the FAO, a fishery is typically defined in terms of the 'people involved, species or type of fish, area of water or seabed, method of fishing, class of boats, purpose of the activities or a combination of the foregoing features'. The definition often includes a combination of fish and fishers in a region, the latter fishing for similar species with similar gear types.
Aquifer	An aquifer is an underground layer of water-bearing permeable rock or unconsolidated materials (gravel, sand, or silt) from which groundwater can be extracted using a water well. The study of water flow in aquifers and the characterization of aquifers is called hydrogeology. Related terms include aquitard, which is a bed of low permeability along an aquifer, and aquiclude, which is a solid, impermeable area underlying or overlying an aquifer.
Groundwater	Groundwater is water located beneath the earth's surface in soil pore spaces and in the fractures of rock formations. A unit of rock or an unconsolidated deposit is called an aquifer when it can yield a usable quantity of water. The depth at which soil pore spaces or fractures and voids in rock become completely saturated with water is called the water table.
Groundwater recharge	Groundwater recharge is a hydrologic process where water moves downward from surface water to groundwater. This process usually occurs in the vadose zone below plant roots and is often expressed as a flux to the water table surface. Recharge occurs both naturally (through the water cycle) and anthropologically (i.e., 'artificial groundwater recharge'), where rainwater and or reclaimed water is routed to the subsurface.
Water table	The water table is the surface where the water pressure head is equal to the atmospheric pressure (where gauge pressure = 0). It may be conveniently visualized as the 'surface' of the subsurface materials that are saturated with groundwater in a given vicinity. However, saturated conditions may extend above the water table as surface tension holds water in some pores below atmospheric pressure.
Saltwater intrusion	Saltwater intrusion is the movement of saline water into freshwater aquifers. Most often, it is caused by ground-water pumping from coastal wells, or from construction of navigation channels or oil field canals. The channels and canals provide conduits for salt water to be brought into fresh water marshes.
Floodplain	A floodplain is an area of land adjacent to a stream or river that stretches from the banks of its channel to the base of the enclosing valley walls and experiences flooding during periods of high discharge. It includes the floodway, which consists of the stream channel and adjacent areas that actively carry flood flows downstream, and the flood fringe, which are areas inundated by the flood, but which do not experience a strong current. In other words, a floodplain is an area near a river or a stream which floods when the water level reaches flood stage.

Visit Cram101.com for full Practice Exams

9. Water Resources

CHAPTER HIGHLIGHTS & NOTES: KEY TERMS, PEOPLE, PLACES, CONCEPTS

Dust Bowl	The Dust Bowl, was a period of severe dust storms causing major ecological and agricultural damage to American and Canadian prairie lands from 1930 to 1936 (in some areas until 1940). The phenomenon was caused by severe drought coupled with decades of extensive farming without crop rotation, fallow fields, cover crops or other techniques to prevent wind erosion. Deep plowing of the virgin topsoil of the Great Plains had displaced the natural deep-rooted grasses that normally kept the soil in place and trapped moisture even during periods of drought and high winds.
Drought	Drought is an extended period of months or years when a region notes a deficiency in its water supply whether surface or underground water. Generally, this occurs when a region receives consistently below average precipitation. It can have a substantial impact on the ecosystem and agriculture of the affected region.
Fish ladder	A fish ladder, fish pass or fish steps, is a structure on or around artificial barriers (such as dams and locks) to facilitate diadromous fishes' natural migration. Most fishways enable fish to pass around the barriers by swimming and leaping up a series of relatively low steps (hence the term ladder) into the waters on the other side. The velocity of water falling over the steps has to be great enough to attract the fish to the ladder, but it cannot be so great that it washes fish back downstream or exhausts them to the point of inability to continue their journey upriver.
Three Gorges Dam	The Three Gorges Dam is a hydroelectric dam that spans the Yangtze River by the town of Sandouping, located in the Yiling District of Yichang, in Hubei province, China. The Three Gorges Dam is the world's largest power station in terms of installed capacity (21,000 MW) but is second to Itaipu Dam with regard to the generation of electricity annually. The dam body was completed in 2006. Except for a ship lift, the originally planned components of the project were completed on October 30, 2008, when the 26th turbine in the shore plant began commercial operation.
Aqueduct	An aqueduct is a watercourse constructed to convey water. In modern engineering, the term aqueduct is used for any system of pipes, ditches, canals, tunnels, and other structures used for this purpose. The term aqueduct also often refers specifically to a bridge on an artificial watercourse.
Colorado River Aqueduct	The Colorado River Aqueduct, is a 242 mi (389 km) water conveyance in Southern California in the United States, operated by the Metropolitan Water District of Southern California (MWD). The aqueduct impounds water from the Colorado River at Lake Havasu on the California-Arizona border west across the Mojave and Colorado deserts to the east side of the Santa Ana Mountains. It is one of the primary sources of drinking water for Southern California.
Desalination	Desalination, desalinization, or desalinisation refers to any of several processes that remove some amount of salt and other minerals from saline water. More generally, desalination may also refer to the removal of salts and minerals, as in soil desalination.

Visit Cram101.com for full Practice Exams

9. Water Resources

CHAPTER HIGHLIGHTS & NOTES: KEY TERMS, PEOPLE, PLACES, CONCEPTS

Distillation	Distillation is a method of separating mixtures based on differences in volatilities of components in a boiling liquid mixture. Distillation is a unit operation, or a physical separation process, and not a chemical reaction. Commercially, distillation has a number of applications.
Reverse osmosis	Reverse osmosis is a purification technology that uses a semi-permeable membrane. This membrane-technology is not properly a filtration method. In RO, an applied pressure is used to overcome osmotic pressure, a colligative properties, that is driven by chemical potential, a thermodynamic parameter.
Drip irrigation	Drip irrigation, is an irrigation method which saves water and fertilizer by allowing water to drip slowly to the roots of plants, either onto the soil surface or directly onto the root zone, through a network of valves, pipes, tubing, and emitters.It is done with the help of narrow tubes which deliver water directly to the base of the plant. Heda irrigation has been used since ancient times when buried clay pots were filled with water, which would gradually seep into the grass. Modern drip irrigation began its development in Afghanistan in 1866 when researchers began experimenting with irrigation using clay pipe to create combination irrigation and drainage systems.
Conservation	Conservation is an ethic of resour use, allocation, and protection. Its primary focus is upon maintaining the health of the natural world: its, fisheries, habitats, and biological diversity. Secondary focus is on materials conservation and energy conservation, which are seen as important to protect the natural world.
Water right	Water right in water law refers to the right of a user to use water from a water source, e.g., a river, stream, pond or source of groundwater. In areas with plentiful water and few users, such systems are generally not complicated or contentious. In other areas, especially arid areas where irrigation is practiced, such systems are often the source of conflict, both legal and physical.

Visit Cram101.com for full Practice Exams

9. Water Resources

CHAPTER QUIZ: KEY TERMS, PEOPLE, PLACES, CONCEPTS

1. _____ is the movement of saline water into freshwater aquifers. Most often, it is caused by ground-water pumping from coastal wells, or from construction of navigation channels or oil field canals. The channels and canals provide conduits for salt water to be brought into fresh water marshes.

   a. Bank
   b. Saltwater intrusion
   c. Buffer strip
   d. Climarice

2. _____ is a hydrologic process where water moves downward from surface water to groundwater. This process usually occurs in the vadose zone below plant roots and is often expressed as a flux to the water table surface. Recharge occurs both naturally (through the water cycle) and anthropologically (i.e., 'artificial _____'), where rainwater and or reclaimed water is routed to the subsurface.

   a. Juglone
   b. Heavy equipment
   c. High strain dynamic testing
   d. Groundwater recharge

3. Generally, a _____ is an entity engaged in raising or harvesting fish which is determined by some authority to be a _____. According to the FAO, a _____ is typically defined in terms of the 'people involved, species or type of fish, area of water or seabed, method of fishing, class of boats, purpose of the activities or a combination of the foregoing features'. The definition often includes a combination of fish and fishers in a region, the latter fishing for similar species with similar gear types.

   a. Fishery
   b. Marine biology
   c. lentic
   d. Juglone

4. An _____ is an underground layer of water-bearing permeable rock or unconsolidated materials (gravel, sand, or silt) from which groundwater can be extracted using a water well. The study of water flow in _____s and the characterization of _____s is called hydrogeology. Related terms include aquitard, which is a bed of low permeability along an _____, and aquiclude, which is a solid, impermeable area underlying or overlying an _____.

   a. Outburst flood
   b. Estuary
   c. Inland sea
   d. Aquifer

5. . A _____, fish pass or fish steps, is a structure on or around artificial barriers (such as dams and locks) to facilitate diadromous fishes' natural migration. Most fishways enable fish to pass around the barriers by swimming and leaping up a series of relatively low steps (hence the term ladder) into the waters on the other side.

Visit Cram101.com for full Practice Exams

9. Water Resources

CHAPTER QUIZ: KEY TERMS, PEOPLE, PLACES, CONCEPTS

The velocity of water falling over the steps has to be great enough to attract the fish to the ladder, but it cannot be so great that it washes fish back downstream or exhausts them to the point of inability to continue their journey upriver.

a. Barrage
b. Brandon Road Lock and Dam Historic District
c. Bunding
d. Fish ladder

Visit Cram101.com for full Practice Exams

Visit Cram101.com for full Practice Exams

ANSWER KEY
9. Water Resources

1. b
2. d
3. a
4. d
5. d

You can take the complete Chapter Practice Test

for 9. Water Resources
on all key terms, persons, places, and concepts.

Online 99 Cents

http://www.epub89.16.23086.9.cram101.com/

Use www.Cram101.com for all your study needs

including Cram101's online interactive problem solving labs in

chemistry, statistics, mathematics, and more.

Visit Cram101.com for full Practice Exams

10. Land, Public and Private

CHAPTER OUTLINE: KEY TERMS, PEOPLE, PLACES, CONCEPTS

Land use

Tragedy of the commons

Externality

Maximum sustainable yield

National park

Land management

Deforestation

Reforestation

Clean Air Act

Clean Water Act

Endangered Species Act

National Environmental Policy Act

Urban sprawl

Smart growth

Infill

Sense of place

Urban growth boundary

Visit Cram101.com for full Practice Exams

10. Land, Public and Private

CHAPTER HIGHLIGHTS & NOTES: KEY TERMS, PEOPLE, PLACES, CONCEPTS

Land use	'Land use' is also often used to refer to the distinct land use types in zoning. Land use is the human use of land. Land use involves the management and modification of natural environment or wilderness into built environment such as fields, pastures, and settlements. It also has been defined as 'the arrangements, activities and inputs people undertake in a certain land cover type to produce, change or maintain it' (FAO, 1997a; FAO/UNEP, 1999).
Tragedy of the commons	The tragedy of the commons is a dilemma arising from the situation in which multiple individuals, acting independently and rationally consulting their own self-interest, will ultimately deplete a shared limited resource, even when it is clear that it is not in anyone's long-term interest for this to happen Central to Hardin's article is an example (first sketched in an 1833 pamphlet by William Forster Lloyd) involving medieval land tenure in Europe, of herders sharing a common parcel of land, on which they are each entitled to let their cows graze.
Externality	In economics, an externality, is a cost or benefit not transmitted through prices that is incurred by a party who did not agree to the action causing the cost or benefit. The cost of an externality is a negative externality, or external cost, while the benefit of an externality is a positive externality, or external benefit. In the case of both negative and positive externalities, prices in a competitive market do not reflect the full costs or benefits of producing or consuming a product or service.
Maximum sustainable yield	In population ecology and economics, maximum sustainable yield is theoretically, the largest yield that can be taken from a species' stock over an indefinite period. Fundamental to the notion of sustainable harvest, the concept of Maximum sustainable yield aims to maintain the population size at the point of maximum growth rate by harvesting the individuals that would normally be added to the population, allowing the population to continue to be productive indefinitely. Under the assumption of logistic growth, resource limitation does not constrain individuals' reproductive rates when populations are small, but because there are few individuals, the overall yield is small.
National park	A national park is a reserve of natural, semi-natural, or developed land that a sovereign state declares or owns. Although individual nations designate their own national parks differently , an international organization, the International Union for Conservation of Nature (IUCN), and its World Commission on Protected Areas, has defined National Parks as its category II type of protected areas.
Land management	Land management is the process of managing the use and development (in both urban and rural settings) of land resources. Land resources are used for a variety of purposes which may include organic agriculture, reforestation, water resource management and eco-tourism projects.

Visit Cram101.com for full Practice Exams

10. Land, Public and Private

CHAPTER HIGHLIGHTS & NOTES: KEY TERMS, PEOPLE, PLACES, CONCEPTS

Deforestation	Deforestation, clearance or clearing is the removal of a forest or stand of trees where the land is thereafter converted to a non-forest use. Examples of deforestation include conversion of forestland to farms, ranches, or urban use. More than half of the animal and plant species in the world live in tropical forests.
Reforestation	Reforestation is the natural or intentional restocking of existing forests and woodlands that have been depleted, usually through deforestation. Reforestation can be used to improve the quality of human life by soaking up pollution and dust from the air, rebuild natural habitats and ecosystems, mitigate global warming since forests facilitate biosequestration of atmospheric carbon dioxide, and harvest for resources, particularly timber. The term reforestation is similar to afforestation, the process of restoring and recreating areas of woodlands or forests that may have existed long ago but were deforested or otherwise removed at some point in the past.
Clean Air Act	The Clean Air Act is a United States federal law designed to control air pollution on a national level. It requires the Environmental Protection Agency (EPA) to develop and enforce regulations to protect the public from airborne contaminants known to be hazardous to human health. The 1963 version of the legislation established a research program, expanded in 1967. Major amendments to the law, requiring regulatory controls for air pollution, passed in 1970, 1977 and 1990.
Clean Water Act	The Clean Water Act is the primary federal law in the United States governing water pollution. Commonly abbreviated as the Clean Water Act, the act established the goals of eliminating releases of high amounts of toxic substances into water, eliminating additional water pollution by 1985, and ensuring that surface waters would meet standards necessary for human sports and recreation by 1983. The principal body of law currently in effect is based on the Federal Water Pollution Control Amendments of 1972 and was significantly expanded from the Federal Water Pollution Control Amendments of 1948. Major amendments were enacted in the Clean Water Act of 1977 and the Water Quality Act of 1987.
Endangered Species Act	The Endangered Species Act of 1973 (Endangered Species Act; 7 U.S.C. § 136, 16 U.S.C. § 1531 et seq). is one of the dozens of United States environmental laws passed in the 1970s. Signed into law by President Richard Nixon on December 28, 1973, it was designed to protect critically imperiled species from extinction as a 'consequence of economic growth and development untempered by adequate concern and conservation.' The Act is administered by two federal agencies, the United States Fish and Wildlife Service (FWS) and the National Oceanic and Atmospheric Administration (NOAA).

Visit Cram101.com for full Practice Exams

10. Land, Public and Private

CHAPTER HIGHLIGHTS & NOTES: KEY TERMS, PEOPLE, PLACES, CONCEPTS

National Environmental Policy Act	The National Environmental Policy Act is a United States environmental law that established a U.S. national policy promoting the enhancement of the environment and also established the President's Council on Environmental Quality (CEQ). Eccleston writes that as one of the most emulated statutes in the world, National Environmental Policy Act has been called the modern day equivalent of an 'Environmental Magna Carta.' National Environmental Policy Act's most significant effect was to set up procedural requirements for all federal government agencies to prepare Environmental Assessments (EAs) and Environmental Impact Statements (EISs). EAs and EISs contain statements of the environmental effects of proposed federal agency actions.
Urban sprawl	Urban sprawl, is a multifaceted concept, which includes the spreading outwards of a city and its suburbs to its outskirts to low-density and auto-dependent development on rural land, high segregation of es (e.g. stores and residential), and vario design features that encourage car dependency. Discsions and debates about sprawl are often obfcated by the ambiguity associated with the phrase. For example, some commentators measure sprawl only with the average number of residential units per acre in a given area.
Smart growth	Smart growth is an urban planning and transportation theory that concentrates growth in compact walkable urban centers to avoid sprawl and advocates compact, transit-oriented, walkable, bicycle-friendly land use, including neighborhood schools, complete streets, and mixed-use development with a range of housing choices. The term 'smart growth' is particularly used in North America. In Europe and particularly the UK, the terms 'Compact City' or 'urban intensification' have often been used to describe similar concepts, which have influenced Government planning policies in the UK, the Netherlands and several other European countries.
Infill	In urban planning, infill is the introduction of new land uses such as housing. Urban infill In the urban planning and development industries, infill is the use of land within a built-up area for further construction, especially as part of a community redevelopment or growth management program or as part of smart growth. It focuses on the reuse and repositioning of obsolete or underutilized buildings and sites.
Sense of place	The term sense of place has been defined and used in many different ways by many different people. To some, it is a characteristic that some geographic places have and some do not, while to others it is a feeling or perception held by people (not by the place itself). It is often used in relation to those characteristics that make a place special or unique, as well as to those that foster a sense of authentic human attachment and belonging.

Visit Cram101.com for full Practice Exams

10. Land, Public and Private

CHAPTER HIGHLIGHTS & NOTES: KEY TERMS, PEOPLE, PLACES, CONCEPTS

Urban growth boundary	An urban growth boundary, is a regional boundary, set in an attempt to control urban sprawl by mandating that the area inside the boundary be used for higher density urban development and the area outside be used for lower density development. An urban growth boundary circumscribes an entire urbanized area and is used by local governments as a guide to zoning and land use decisions. If the area affected by the boundary includes multiple jurisdictions a special urban planning agency may be created by the state or regional government to manage the boundary.

CHAPTER QUIZ: KEY TERMS, PEOPLE, PLACES, CONCEPTS

1. In urban planning, _____ is the introduction of new land uses such as housing. Urban _____

    In the urban planning and development industries, _____ is the use of land within a built-up area for further construction, especially as part of a community redevelopment or growth management program or as part of smart growth. It focuses on the reuse and repositioning of obsolete or underutilized buildings and sites.

    a. Infill
    b. Oedometer test
    c. Asher Shadmon
    d. Unified Soil Classification System

2. The _____ is a United States environmental law that established a U.S. national policy promoting the enhancement of the environment and also established the President's Council on Environmental Quality (CEQ). Eccleston writes that as one of the most emulated statutes in the world, _____ has been called the modern day equivalent of an 'Environmental Magna Carta.'

    _____'s most significant effect was to set up procedural requirements for all federal government agencies to prepare Environmental Assessments (EAs) and Environmental Impact Statements (EISs). EAs and EISs contain statements of the environmental effects of proposed federal agency actions.

    a. Juglone
    b. Gibbons v. Ogden
    c. National Environmental Policy Act
    d. runoff

3. . The _____ is the primary federal law in the United States governing water pollution.

Visit Cram101.com for full Practice Exams

10. Land, Public and Private

CHAPTER QUIZ: KEY TERMS, PEOPLE, PLACES, CONCEPTS

Commonly abbreviated as the _____, the act established the goals of eliminating releases of high amounts of toxic substances into water, eliminating additional water pollution by 1985, and ensuring that surface waters would meet standards necessary for human sports and recreation by 1983.

The principal body of law currently in effect is based on the Federal Water Pollution Control Amendments of 1972 and was significantly expanded from the Federal Water Pollution Control Amendments of 1948. Major amendments were enacted in the _____ of 1977 and the Water Quality Act of 1987.

a. Federal Insecticide, Fungicide, and Rodenticide Act
b. Juglone
c. Clean Water Act
d. runoff

4. _____ is an urban planning and transportation theory that concentrates growth in compact walkable urban centers to avoid sprawl and advocates compact, transit-oriented, walkable, bicycle-friendly land use, including neighborhood schools, complete streets, and mixed-use development with a range of housing choices. The term '_____' is particularly used in North America. In Europe and particularly the UK, the terms 'Compact City' or 'urban intensification' have often been used to describe similar concepts, which have influenced Government planning policies in the UK, the Netherlands and several other European countries.

a. Biodiesel
b. cycling
c. Juglone
d. Smart growth

5. '_____' is also often used to refer to the distinct _____ types in zoning.

_____ is the human use of land. _____ involves the management and modification of natural environment or wilderness into built environment such as fields, pastures, and settlements. It also has been defined as 'the arrangements, activities and inputs people undertake in a certain land cover type to produce, change or maintain it' (FAO, 1997a; FAO/UNEP, 1999).

a. Juglone
b. Gibbons v. Ogden
c. Krakatoa
d. Land use

Visit Cram101.com for full Practice Exams

Visit Cram101.com for full Practice Exams

ANSWER KEY
10. Land, Public and Private

1. a

2. c

3. c

4. d

5. d

You can take the complete Chapter Practice Test

for 10. Land, Public and Private
on all key terms, persons, places, and concepts.

Online 99 Cents

http://www.epub89.16.23086.10.cram101.com/

Use www.Cram101.com for all your study needs

including Cram101's online interactive problem solving labs in

chemistry, statistics, mathematics, and more.

Visit Cram101.com for full Practice Exams

11. Feeding the World

CHAPTER OUTLINE: KEY TERMS, PEOPLE, PLACES, CONCEPTS

Anemia

Food security

Overnutrition

Industrial agriculture

Economies of scale

Waterlogging

Bioaccumulation

Herbicide

Insecticide

Pesticide

Protozoa

Roundup

Genetically modified organism

Crop rotation

Desertification

Intercropping

Sustainable agriculture

Agroforestry

Contour plowing

Degradation

Integrated pest management

Visit Cram101.com for full Practice Exams

11. Feeding the World

CHAPTER OUTLINE: KEY TERMS, PEOPLE, PLACES, CONCEPTS

Concentrated Animal Feeding Operation

Feedlot

Aquaculture

Fishery

Tragedy of the commons

Bycatch

CHAPTER HIGHLIGHTS & NOTES: KEY TERMS, PEOPLE, PLACES, CONCEPTS

Anemia

Anemia is a decrease in number of red blood cells (RBCs) or less than the normal quantity of hemoglobin in the blood. However, it can include decreased oxygen-binding ability of each hemoglobin molecule due to deformity or lack in numerical development as in some other types of hemoglobin deficiency. Because hemoglobin (found inside RBCs) normally carries oxygen from the lungs to the capillaries, anemia leads to hypoxia (lack of oxygen) in organs.

Food security

Food security refers to the availability of food and one's access to it. A household is considered food-secure when its occupants do not live in hunger or fear of starvation. According to the World Resources Institute, global per capita food production has been increasing substantially for the past several decades.

Overnutrition

Overnutrition is a form of malnutrition in which nutrients are oversupplied relative to the amounts required for normal growth, development, and metabolism. Overnutrition is a type of malnutrition where there are more nutrients than required for normal growth.

The term can refer to:•obesity, brought on by general overeating of foods high in caloric content, as well as:•the oversupply of a specific nutrient or categories of nutrients, such as mineral or vitamin poisoning, due to excessive intake of dietary supplements or foods high in nutrients (such as liver), or nutritional imbalances caused by various fad diets.

For mineral excess, see:•Iron poisoning, and•low sodium diet (excess sodium)..

Visit Cram101.com for full Practice Exams

11. Feeding the World

CHAPTER HIGHLIGHTS & NOTES: KEY TERMS, PEOPLE, PLACES, CONCEPTS

Industrial agriculture	Industrial farming is a form of modern farming that refers to the industrialized production of livestock, poultry, fish, and crops. The methods of industrial agriculture are technoscientific, economic, and political. They include innovation in agricultural machinery and farming methods, genetic technology, techniques for achieving economies of scale in production, the creation of new markets for consumption, the application of patent protection to genetic information, and global trade.
Economies of scale	In microeconomics, economies of scale are the cost advantages that an enterprise obtains due to expansion. There are factors that cause a producer's average cost per unit to fall as the scale of output is increased. 'Economies of scale' is a long run concept and refers to reductions in unit cost as the size of a facility and the usage levels of other inputs increase.
Waterlogging	In archaeology, waterlogging refers to the long-term exclusion of air by groundwater. Such waterlogging preserves perishable artifacts. Thus, in a site which has been waterlogged since the archaeological horizon was deposited, exceptional insight may be obtained by study of artifacts made of leather, wood, textile or similar materials.
Bioaccumulation	Bioaccumulation refers to the accumulation of substances, such as pesticides, or other organic chemicals in an organism. Bioaccumulation occurs when an organism absorbs a toxic substance at a rate greater than that at which the substance is lost. Thus, the longer the biological half-life of the substance the greater the risk of chronic poisoning, even if environmental levels of the toxin are not very high.
Herbicide	Herbicides, also commonly known as weedkillers, are pesticides used to kill unwanted plants. Selective herbicides kill specific targets while leaving the desired crop relatively unharmed. Some of these act by interfering with the growth of the weed and are often synthetic 'imitations' of plant hormones.
Insecticide	An insecticide is a pesticide used against insects. They include ovicides and larvicides used against the eggs and larvae of insects respectively. Insecticides are used in agriculture, medicine, industry and the household.
Pesticide	Pesticides are substances meant for preventing, destroying or mitigating any pest. They are a class of biocide. The most common use of pesticides is as plant protection products (also known as crop protection products), which in general protect plants from damaging influences such as weeds, diseases or insects.
Protozoa	Protozoa are a diverse group of unicellular eukaryotic organisms, many of which are motile. Originally, protozoa had been defined as unicellular protists with animal-like behavior, e.g., movement. Protozoa were regarded as the partner group of protists to protophyta, which have plant-like behaviour, e.g., photosynthesis.
Roundup	Roundup is the brand name of a systemic, broad-spectrum herbicide produced by the U.S.

Visit Cram101.com for full Practice Exams

11. Feeding the World

CHAPTER HIGHLIGHTS & NOTES: KEY TERMS, PEOPLE, PLACES, CONCEPTS

	company Monsanto, and contains the active ingredient glyphosate. Glyphosate is the most widely used herbicide in the USA, and Roundup has been the number one selling herbicide worldwide since at least 1980. As of 2009, sales of Roundup herbicides represent about 10% of Monsanto's revenue due to competition from Chinese producers of other glyphosate-based herbicides; the overall Roundup line of products represents about half of Monsanto's yearly revenue. Monsanto developed and patented the glyphosate molecule in the 1970s, and marketed Roundup from 1973. It retained exclusive rights in the US until its US patent expired in September, 2000, and maintained a predominant marketshare in countries where the patent expired earlier.
Genetically modified organism	A genetically modified organism or genetically engineered organism (GEO) is an organism whose genetic material has been altered using genetic engineering techniques. These techniques, generally known as recombinant DNA technology, use DNA molecules from different sources, which are combined into one molecule to create a new set of genes. This DNA is then transferred into an organism, giving it modified or novel genes.
Crop rotation	Crop rotation is the practice of growing a series of dissimilar types of crops in the same area in sequential seasons. Crop rotation confers various benefits to the soil. A traditional element of crop rotation is the replenishment of nitrogen through the use of green manure in sequence with cereals and other crops.
Desertification	Desertification is a type of land degradation in which a relatively dry land region becomes increasingly arid, typically losing its bodies of water as well as vegetation and wildlife. It is caused by a variety of factors, such as climate change and human activities. Desertification is a significant global ecological and environmental problem.
Intercropping	Intercropping is the practice of growing two or more crops in proximity. The most common goal of intercropping is to produce a greater yield on a given piece of land by making use of resources that would otherwise not be utilized by a single crop. Careful planning is required, taking into account the soil, climate, crops, and varieties.
Sustainable agriculture	Sustainable agriculture is the practice of farming using principles of ecology, the study of relationships between organisms and their environment. It has been defined as 'an integrated system of plant and animal production practices having a site-specific application that will last over the long term:•tisfy human food and fiber needs•Enhance environmental quality and the natural resource base upon which the agricultural economy depends•Make the most efficient use of non-renewable resources and on-farm resources and integrate, where appropriate, natural biological cycles and controls•Sustain the economic viability of farm operations•Enhance the quality of life for farmers and society as a whole.'

Visit Cram101.com for full Practice Exams

11. Feeding the World

CHAPTER HIGHLIGHTS & NOTES: KEY TERMS, PEOPLE, PLACES, CONCEPTS

Sustainable agriculture in the United States was addressed by the 1990 farm bill. More recently, as consumer and retail demand for sustainable products has risen, organizations such as Food Alliance and Protected Harvest have started to provide measurement standards and certification programs for what constitutes a sustainably grown crop.

Agroforestry

Agroforestry is an integrated approach of using the interactive benefits from combining trees and shrubs with crops and/or livestock. It combines agricultural and forestry technologies to create more diverse, productive, profitable, healthy and sustainable land-use systems.

According to the World Agroforestry Centre, Agroforestry is a collective name for land use systems and practices in which woody perennials are deliberately integrated with crops and/or animals on the same land management unit.

Contour plowing

Contour plowing or contour farming is the farming practice of plowing across a slope following its elevation contour lines. The rows form slow water run-off during rainstorms to prevent soil erosion and allow the water time to settle into the soil. In contour plowing, the ruts made by the plow run perpendicular rather than parallel to slopes, generally resulting in furrows that curve around the land and are level.

Degradation

In geology, degradation refers to the lowering of a fluvial surface, such as a stream bed or floodplain, through erosional processes. It is the opposite of aggradation. Degradation is characteristic of channel networks in which either bedrock erosion is taking place, or in systems that are sediment-starved and are therefore entraining more material than is being deposited.

Integrated pest management

Integrated pest management also known as Integrated Pest Control (IPC) is a broad based approach that integrates a range of practices for economic control of pests. Integrated pest management aims to suppress pest populations below the economic injury level (EIL). The Food and Agriculture Organisation of the UN defines Integrated pest management as 'the careful consideration of all available pest control techniques and subsequent integration of appropriate measures that discourage the development of pest populations and keep pesticides and other interventions to levels that are economically justified and reduce or minimize risks to human health and the environment.

Concentrated Animal Feeding Operation

A Concentrated Animal Feeding Operation is a term that was first coined by the United States' Environmental Protection Agency (EPA) to describe animal agricultural facilities that have a potential pollution profile. Specifically, the EPA defines a Concentrated Animal Feeding Operation as an animal feeding operation (AFO) that (a) confines animals for more than 45 days during a growing season, (b) in an area that does not produce vegetation, and (c) meets certain size thresholds.

Visit Cram101.com for full Practice Exams

11. Feeding the World

CHAPTER HIGHLIGHTS & NOTES: KEY TERMS, PEOPLE, PLACES, CONCEPTS

The EPA's definition of the term 'captures key elements of the transformations' observed in the animal agriculture sector over the course of the 20th century: 'a production process that concentrates large numbers of animals in relatively small and confined places, and that substitutes structures and equipment (for feeding, temperature controls, and manure management) for land and labor.'

There are roughly 257,000 AFOs in the United States, of which 15,500 meet the more narrow criteria for Concentrated Animal Feeding Operations.

Feedlot

A feedlot is a type of animal feeding operation (AFO) which is used in factory farming for finishing livestock, notably beef cattle, but also swine, horses, sheep, turkeys, chickens or ducks, prior to slaughter. Large beef feedlots are called Concentrated Animal Feeding Operations (CAFOs). They may contain thousands of animals in an array of pens.

Aquaculture

Aquaculture, is the farming of aquatic organisms such as fish, crustaceans, molluscs and aquatic plants. Aquaculture involves cultivating freshwater and saltwater populations under controlled conditions, and can be contrasted with commercial fishing, which is the harvesting of wild fish. Mariculture refers to aquaculture practised in marine environments.

Fishery

Generally, a fishery is an entity engaged in raising or harvesting fish which is determined by some authority to be a fishery. According to the FAO, a fishery is typically defined in terms of the 'people involved, species or type of fish, area of water or seabed, method of fishing, class of boats, purpose of the activities or a combination of the foregoing features'. The definition often includes a combination of fish and fishers in a region, the latter fishing for similar species with similar gear types.

Tragedy of the commons

The tragedy of the commons is a dilemma arising from the situation in which multiple individuals, acting independently and rationally consulting their own self-interest, will ultimately deplete a shared limited resource, even when it is clear that it is not in anyone's long-term interest for this to happen

Central to Hardin's article is an example (first sketched in an 1833 pamphlet by William Forster Lloyd) involving medieval land tenure in Europe, of herders sharing a common parcel of land, on which they are each entitled to let their cows graze.

Bycatch

The term 'bycatch' is usually used for fish caught unintentionally in a fishery while intending to catch other fish. It may however also indicate untargeted catch in other forms of animal harvesting or collecting. Bycatch is of a different species, undersized individuals of the target species, or juveniles of the target species.

Visit Cram101.com for full Practice Exams

11. Feeding the World

103

CHAPTER QUIZ: KEY TERMS, PEOPLE, PLACES, CONCEPTS

1. _____ refers to the availability of food and one's access to it. A household is considered food-secure when its occupants do not live in hunger or fear of starvation. According to the World Resources Institute, global per capita food production has been increasing substantially for the past several decades.

   a. Food security
   b. Food waste in New Zealand
   c. Food waste in the United Kingdom
   d. Pesticide residue

2. _____ is a decrease in number of red blood cells (RBCs) or less than the normal quantity of hemoglobin in the blood. However, it can include decreased oxygen-binding ability of each hemoglobin molecule due to deformity or lack in numerical development as in some other types of hemoglobin deficiency. Because hemoglobin (found inside RBCs) normally carries oxygen from the lungs to the capillaries, _____ leads to hypoxia (lack of oxygen) in organs.

   a. Anemia
   b. Endangered Species Act
   c. United Nations Framework Convention on Climate Change
   d. Absent-minded professor

3. _____s are substances meant for preventing, destroying or mitigating any pest. They are a class of biocide. The most common use of _____s is as plant protection products (also known as crop protection products), which in general protect plants from damaging influences such as weeds, diseases or insects.

   a. Pesticide poisoning
   b. Juglone
   c. Pesticide
   d. Methyl tert-butyl ether

4. A _____ or genetically engineered organism (GEO) is an organism whose genetic material has been altered using genetic engineering techniques. These techniques, generally known as recombinant DNA technology, use DNA molecules from different sources, which are combined into one molecule to create a new set of genes. This DNA is then transferred into an organism, giving it modified or novel genes.

   a. Biosafety Clearing-House
   b. Genetically modified organism
   c. Blue rose
   d. Gene knockdown

5. . _____ or contour farming is the farming practice of plowing across a slope following its elevation contour lines. The rows form slow water run-off during rainstorms to prevent soil erosion and allow the water time to settle into the soil. In _____, the ruts made by the plow run perpendicular rather than parallel to slopes, generally resulting in furrows that curve around the land and are level.

   a. Cover crop

Visit Cram101.com for full Practice Exams

11. Feeding the World

CHAPTER QUIZ: KEY TERMS, PEOPLE, PLACES, CONCEPTS

b. Crop rotation

c. Drainage equation

d. Contour plowing

Visit Cram101.com for full Practice Exams

Visit Cram101.com for full Practice Exams

ANSWER KEY
11. Feeding the World

1. a
2. a
3. c
4. b
5. d

You can take the complete Chapter Practice Test

for 11. Feeding the World
on all key terms, persons, places, and concepts.

Online 99 Cents

http://www.epub89.16.23086.11.cram101.com/

Use www.Cram101.com for all your study needs

including Cram101's online interactive problem solving labs in

chemistry, statistics, mathematics, and more.

Visit Cram101.com for full Practice Exams

12. Nonrenewable Energy Sources

CHAPTER OUTLINE: KEY TERMS, PEOPLE, PLACES, CONCEPTS

Fossil fuel

Embodied energy

Energy carrier

Cogeneration

Bituminous coal

Peat

Sub-bituminous coal

Asphalt

Oil sands

Hubbert curve

M. King Hubbert

Peak oil

Binary fission

Radioactive decay

Radioactive waste

Nuclear fusion

Yucca Mountain

Visit Cram101.com for full Practice Exams

12. Nonrenewable Energy Sources

CHAPTER HIGHLIGHTS & NOTES: KEY TERMS, PEOPLE, PLACES, CONCEPTS

Fossil fuel	Fossil fuels are fuels formed by natural processes such as anaerobic decomposition of buried dead organisms. The age of the organisms and their resulting fossil fuels is typically millions of years, and sometimes exceeds 650 million years. Fossil fuels contain high percentages of carbon and include coal, petroleum, and natural gas.
Embodied energy	Embodied Energy is the sum of all the energy required to produce goods or services, considered as if that energy was incorporated or 'embodied' in the product itself. The concept can be useful in determining the effectiveness of energy-producing or energy-saving devices, of buildings, and, because energy-inputs usually entail greenhouse gas emissions, in deciding whether a product contributes to or mitigates global warming. Embodied energy is an accounting method which aims to find the sum total of the energy necessary for an entire product life-cycle.
Energy carrier	According to ISO 13600, an energy carrier is either a substance (energy form) or a phenomenon (energy system) that can be used to produce mhanical work or heat or to operate chemical or physical processes. In the field of Energetics, however, an energy carrier corresponds only to an energy form (not an energy system) of energy input required by the various stors of society to perform their functions. Examples of energy carriers include liquid fuel in a furnace, gasoline in a pump, eltricity in a factory or a house, and hydrogen in a tank of a car.
Cogeneration	Cogeneration is the use of a heat engine or a power station to simultaneously generate both electricity and useful heat. All thermal power plants emit a certain amount of heat during electricity generation. This can be released into the natural environment through cooling towers, flue gas, or by other means. By contrast, cogeneration captures some or all of the by-product heat for heating purposes, either very close to the plant, or-especially in Scandinavia and eastern Europe-as hot water for district heating with temperatures ranging from approximately 80 to 130 °C.
Bituminous coal	Bituminous coal is a relatively soft coal containing a tarlike substance called bitumen. It is of higher quality than lignite coal but of poorer quality than anthracite. It was usually formed as a result of high pressure on lignite.
Peat	Peat is an accumulation of partially decayed vegetation. One of the most common components is Sphagnum moss, although many other plants can contribute. Soils that contain mostly peat are known as a histosol.

Visit Cram101.com for full Practice Exams

12. Nonrenewable Energy Sources

CHAPTER HIGHLIGHTS & NOTES: KEY TERMS, PEOPLE, PLACES, CONCEPTS

Sub-bituminous coal	Sub-bituminous coal is a type of coal whose properties range from those of lignite to those of bituminous coal and are used primarily as fuel for steam-electric power generation.
	Sub-bituminous coals may be dull, dark brown to black, soft and crumbly at the lower end of the range, to bright jet-black, hard, and relatively strong at the upper end. They contain 15-30% inherent moisture by weight and are non-coking (undergo little swelling upon heating).
Asphalt	Asphalt or or, also known as bitumen, is a sticky, black and highly viscous liquid or semi-solid form of petroleum. It may be found in natural deposits or may be a refined product; it is a substance classed as a pitch. Until the 20th century, the term asphaltum was also used.
Oil sands	Bituminous sands, colloquially known as oil sands, are a type of unconventional petroleum deposit. The sands contain naturally occurring mixtures of sand, clay, water, and a dense and extremely viscous form of petroleum technically referred to as bitumen (or colloquially 'tar' due to its similar appearance, odour, and colour). Oil sands are found in large amounts in many countries throughout the world, but are found in extremely large quantities in Canada and Venezuela.
Hubbert curve	The Hubbert curve is an approximation of the production rate of a resource over time. It is a symmetric logistic distribution curve, often confused with the 'normal' gaussian function. It first appeared in 'Nuclear Energy and the Fossil Fuels,' geologist M. King Hubbert's 1956 presentation to the American Petroleum Institute, as an idealized symmetric curve, during his tenure at the Shell Oil Company.
M. King Hubbert	Marion King Hubbert (October 5, 1903 - October 11, 1989) was a geoscientist who worked at the Shell research lab in Houston, Texas. He made several important contributions to geology, geophysics, and petroleum geology, most notably the Hubbert curve and Hubbert peak theory (a basic component of Peak oil), with important political ramifications. He was often referred to as 'M. King Hubbert' or 'King Hubbert'.
Peak oil	Peak oil is the point in time when the maximum rate of petroleum extraction is reached, after which the rate of production is expected to enter terminal decline. Global production of oil fell from a high point in 2005 at 74 mb/d, but has since rebounded, and 2011 figures show slightly higher levels of production than in 2005. There is active debate as to how to measure peak oil, and which types of liquid fuels to include. Most of the remaining oil is from unconventional sources.
Binary fission	In biology, fission is the subdivision of a cell into two or more parts and the regeneration of those parts into separate cells (bodies, populations, or species). Binary fission produces two separate cells, populations, species, etc., whereas multiple fission produces more than two cells, populations, species, etc.

Visit Cram101.com for full Practice Exams

12. Nonrenewable Energy Sources

CHAPTER HIGHLIGHTS & NOTES: KEY TERMS, PEOPLE, PLACES, CONCEPTS

Radioactive decay	Radioactive decay is the process by which an atomic nucleus of an unstable atom loses energy by emitting ionizing particles (ionizing radiation) A decay, or loss of energy, results when an atom with one type of nucleus, called the parent radionuclide, transforms to an atom with a nucleus in a different state, or to a different nucleus containing different numbers of nucleons.
Radioactive waste	Radioactive wastes are wastes that contain radioactive material. Radioactive wastes are usually by -products of nuclear power generation and other applications of nuclear fission or nuclear technology, such as research and medicine. Radioactive waste is hazardous to most forms of life and the environment, and is regulated by government agencies in order to protect human health and the environment.
Nuclear fusion	Nuclear fusion is the process by which two or more atomic nuclei join together, or 'fuse', to form a single heavier nucleus. This is usually accompanied by the release or absorption of large quantities of energy. Fusion is the process that powers active stars, the hydrogen bomb and some experimental devices examining fusion power for electrical generation.
Yucca Mountain	Yucca Mountain is a mountain in Nevada, near its border with California, approximately 100 miles (160 km) northwest of Las Vegas. Located in the Great Basin, Yucca Mountain is east of Amargosa Desert, south of the Nevada Test and Training Range and in the Nevada Test Site. It was the site for the Yucca Mountain nuclear waste repository before that plan was scrapped in 2010.

CHAPTER QUIZ: KEY TERMS, PEOPLE, PLACES, CONCEPTS

1. Bituminous sands, colloquially known as _____, are a type of unconventional petroleum deposit. The sands contain naturally occurring mixtures of sand, clay, water, and a dense and extremely viscous form of petroleum technically referred to as bitumen (or colloquially 'tar' due to its similar appearance, odour, and colour). _____ are found in large amounts in many countries throughout the world, but are found in extremely large quantities in Canada and Venezuela.

   a. Juglone
   b. Oil sands
   c. Enthalpy of mixing
   d. Enthalpy of sublimation

2. . _____s are fuels formed by natural processes such as anaerobic decomposition of buried dead organisms. The age of the organisms and their resulting _____s is typically millions of years, and sometimes exceeds 650 million years. _____s contain high percentages of carbon and include coal, petroleum, and natural gas.

   a. Fossil fuel
   b. Juglone

Visit Cram101.com for full Practice Exams

12. Nonrenewable Energy Sources

CHAPTER QUIZ: KEY TERMS, PEOPLE, PLACES, CONCEPTS

  c. Gibbons v. Ogden
  d. Krakatoa

3. Marion King Hubbert (October 5, 1903 - October 11, 1989) was a geoscientist who worked at the Shell research lab in Houston, Texas. He made several important contributions to geology, geophysics, and petroleum geology, most notably the Hubbert curve and Hubbert peak theory (a basic component of Peak oil), with important political ramifications. He was often referred to as '_____' or 'King Hubbert'.

  a. M. King Hubbert
  b. Energy value of coal
  c. Enthalpy of mixing
  d. Enthalpy of sublimation

4. _____ is a type of coal whose properties range from those of lignite to those of bituminous coal and are used primarily as fuel for steam-electric power generation.

  _____s may be dull, dark brown to black, soft and crumbly at the lower end of the range, to bright jet-black, hard, and relatively strong at the upper end. They contain 15-30% inherent moisture by weight and are non-coking (undergo little swelling upon heating).

  a. Sub-bituminous coal
  b. Energy value of coal
  c. Enthalpy of mixing
  d. Enthalpy of sublimation

5. _____ is the use of a heat engine or a power station to simultaneously generate both electricity and useful heat.

  All thermal power plants emit a certain amount of heat during electricity generation. This can be released into the natural environment through cooling towers, flue gas, or by other means. By contrast, _____ captures some or all of the by-product heat for heating purposes, either very close to the plant, or-especially in Scandinavia and eastern Europe-as hot water for district heating with temperatures ranging from approximately 80 to 130 °C.

  a. Combined heat and power
  b. Energy value of coal
  c. Cogeneration
  d. Enthalpy of sublimation

Visit Cram101.com for full Practice Exams

Visit Cram101.com for full Practice Exams

ANSWER KEY
12. Nonrenewable Energy Sources

1. b
2. a
3. a
4. a
5. c

You can take the complete Chapter Practice Test

for 12. Nonrenewable Energy Sources
on all key terms, persons, places, and concepts.

Online 99 Cents

http://www.epub89.16.23086.12.cram101.com/

Use www.Cram101.com for all your study needs

including Cram101's online interactive problem solving labs in

chemistry, statistics, mathematics, and more.

Visit Cram101.com for full Practice Exams

13. Achieving Energy Sustainability

CHAPTER OUTLINE: KEY TERMS, PEOPLE, PLACES, CONCEPTS

_____ Tidal energy

_____ Renewable energy

_____ Energy conservation

_____ Sustainable design

_____ Biofuel

_____ Biomass

_____ Biodiesel

_____ Ethanol

_____ Hydroelectricity

_____ Three Gorges Dam

_____ Fish ladder

_____ Siltation

_____ Solar energy

_____ Solar cell

_____ Geothermal energy

_____ Wind turbine

_____ Electrolysis

_____ Cellulosic ethanol

Visit Cram101.com for full Practice Exams

13. Achieving Energy Sustainability

CHAPTER HIGHLIGHTS & NOTES: KEY TERMS, PEOPLE, PLACES, CONCEPTS

Tidal energy	Tidal power, also called tidal energy, is a form of hydropower that converts the energy of tides into useful forms of power - mainly electricity. Although not yet widely used, tidal power has potential for future electricity generation. Tides are more predictable than wind energy and solar power.
Renewable energy	Renewable energy is energy that comes from natural resources such as sunlight, wind, rain, tides, waves and geothermal heat, which are renewable because they are naturally replenished at a constant rate. About 16% of global final energy consumption comes from renewables, with 10% coming from traditional biomass, which is mainly used for heating, and 3.4% from hydroelectricity. New renewables (small hydro, modern biomass, wind, solar, geothermal, and biofuels) accounted for another 3% and are growing very rapidly.
Energy conservation	Energy conservation refers to reducing energy through using less of an energy service. Energy conservation differs from efficient energy use, which refers to using less energy for a constant service. For example, driving less is an example of energy conservation.
Sustainable design	Sustainable design. is the philosophy of designing physical objects, the built environment, and services to comply with the principles of economic, social, and ecological sustainability. The intention of sustainable design is to 'eliminate negative environmental impact completely through skillful, sensitive design'.
Biofuel	A biofuel is a type of fuel whose energy is derived from biological carbon fixation. Biofuels include fuels derived from biomass conversion, as well as solid biomass, liquid fuels and various biogases. Biofuels are gaining increased public and scientific attention, driven by factors such as oil price hikes and the need for increased energy security.
Biomass	Biomass, in ecology, is the mass of living biological organisms in a given area or ecosystem at a given time. Biomass can refer to species biomass, which is the mass of one or more species, or to community biomass, which is the mass of all species in the community. It can include microorganisms, plants or animals.
Biodiesel	Biodiesel refers to a vegetable oil- or animal fat-based diesel fuel consisting of long-chain alkyl (methyl, propyl or ethyl) esters. Biodiesel is typically made by chemically reacting lipids (e.g., vegetable oil, animal fat (tallow)) with an alcohol producing fatty acid esters. Biodiesel is meant to be used in standard diesel engines and is thus distinct from the vegetable and waste oils used to fuel converted diesel engines.
Ethanol	Ethanol, pure alcohol, grain alcohol, or drinking alcohol, is a volatile, flammable, colorless liquid. It is a psychoactive drug and one of the oldest recreational drugs.

Visit Cram101.com for full Practice Exams

13. Achieving Energy Sustainability

CHAPTER HIGHLIGHTS & NOTES: KEY TERMS, PEOPLE, PLACES, CONCEPTS

Hydroelectricity	Hydroelectricity is the term referring to electricity generated by hydropower; the production of electrical power through the use of the gravitational force of falling or flowing water. It is the most widely used form of renewable energy. Once a hydroelectric complex is constructed, the project produces no direct waste, and has a considerably lower output level of the greenhouse gas carbon dioxide (CO_2) than fossil fuel powered energy plants.
Three Gorges Dam	The Three Gorges Dam is a hydroelectric dam that spans the Yangtze River by the town of Sandouping, located in the Yiling District of Yichang, in Hubei province, China. The Three Gorges Dam is the world's largest power station in terms of installed capacity (21,000 MW) but is second to Itaipu Dam with regard to the generation of electricity annually. The dam body was completed in 2006. Except for a ship lift, the originally planned components of the project were completed on October 30, 2008, when the 26th turbine in the shore plant began commercial operation.
Fish ladder	A fish ladder, fish pass or fish steps, is a structure on or around artificial barriers (such as dams and locks) to facilitate diadromous fishes' natural migration. Most fishways enable fish to pass around the barriers by swimming and leaping up a series of relatively low steps (hence the term ladder) into the waters on the other side. The velocity of water falling over the steps has to be great enough to attract the fish to the ladder, but it cannot be so great that it washes fish back downstream or exhausts them to the point of inability to continue their journey upriver.
Siltation	Siltation is the pollution of water by fine particulate terrestrial clastic material, with a particle size dominated by silt or clay. It refers both to the increased concentration of suspended sediments, and to the increased accumulation (temporary or permanent) of fine sediments on bottoms where they are undesirable. Siltation is most often caused by soil erosion or sediment spill.
Solar energy	Solar energy, radiant light and heat from the sun, has been harnessed by humans since ancient times using a range of ever-evolving technologies. Solar radiation, along with secondary solar-powered resources such as wind and wave power, hydroelectricity and biomass, account for most of the available renewable energy on earth. Only a minuscule fraction of the available solar energy is used.
Solar cell	A solar cell is a solid state electrical device that converts the energy of light directly into electricity by the photovoltaic effect. Assemblies of cells used to make solar modules which are used to capture energy from sunlight, are known as solar panels. The energy generated from these solar modules, referred to as solar power, is an example of solar energy.
Geothermal energy	Geothermal energy is thermal energy generated and stored in the Earth. Thermal energy is the energy that determines the temperature of matter.

Visit Cram101.com for full Practice Exams

13. Achieving Energy Sustainability

CHAPTER HIGHLIGHTS & NOTES: KEY TERMS, PEOPLE, PLACES, CONCEPTS

Wind turbine	A wind turbine is a device that converts kinetic energy from the wind, also called wind energy, into mechanical energy; a process known as wind power. If the mechanical energy is used to produce electricity, the device may be called wind turbine or wind power plant. If the mechanical energy is used to drive machinery, such as for grinding grain or pumping water, the device is called a windmill or wind pump.
Electrolysis	In chemistry and manufacturing, electrolysis is a method of using a direct electric current (DC) to drive an otherwise non-spontaneous chemical reaction. Electrolysis is commercially highly important as a stage in the separation of elements from naturally occurring sources such as ores using an electrolytic cell. The word electrolysis comes from the Greek ?λεκτρον [lýsis] 'dissolution'.
Cellulosic ethanol	Cellulosic ethanol is a biofuel produced from wood, grasses, or the inedible parts of plants. It is a type of biofuel produced from lignocellulose, a structural material that comprises much of the mass of plants. Lignocellulose is composed mainly of cellulose, hemicellulose and lignin.

CHAPTER QUIZ: KEY TERMS, PEOPLE, PLACES, CONCEPTS

1. _____, in ecology, is the mass of living biological organisms in a given area or ecosystem at a given time. _____ can refer to species _____, which is the mass of one or more species, or to community _____, which is the mass of all species in the community. It can include microorganisms, plants or animals.

   a. Biomass
   b. Carbon diet
   c. Climax vegetation
   d. Coevolution

2. . _____ refers to a vegetable oil- or animal fat-based diesel fuel consisting of long-chain alkyl (methyl, propyl or ethyl) esters. _____ is typically made by chemically reacting lipids (e.g., vegetable oil, animal fat (tallow)) with an alcohol producing fatty acid esters.

   _____ is meant to be used in standard diesel engines and is thus distinct from the vegetable and waste oils used to fuel converted diesel engines.

   a. Juglone
   b. Biodiesel
   c. Climax vegetation

Visit Cram101.com for full Practice Exams

13. Achieving Energy Sustainability

CHAPTER QUIZ: KEY TERMS, PEOPLE, PLACES, CONCEPTS

3. _____. is the philosophy of designing physical objects, the built environment, and services to comply with the principles of economic, social, and ecological sustainability.

The intention of _____ is to 'eliminate negative environmental impact completely through skillful, sensitive design'.

a. Sustainable distribution
b. Sustainable design
c. Sustainable forest management
d. Sustainable furniture design

4. _____, radiant light and heat from the sun, has been harnessed by humans since ancient times using a range of ever-evolving technologies. Solar radiation, along with secondary solar-powered resources such as wind and wave power, hydroelectricity and biomass, account for most of the available renewable energy on earth. Only a minuscule fraction of the available _____ is used.

a. Solar water heating
b. Juglone
c. Gibbons v. Ogden
d. Solar energy

5. Tidal power, also called _____, is a form of hydropower that converts the energy of tides into useful forms of power - mainly electricity.

Although not yet widely used, tidal power has potential for future electricity generation. Tides are more predictable than wind energy and solar power.

a. Head of tide
b. Tidal energy
c. King tide
d. Perigean spring tide

Visit Cram101.com for full Practice Exams

Visit Cram101.com for full Practice Exams

ANSWER KEY
13. Achieving Energy Sustainability

1. a

2. b

3. b

4. d

5. b

You can take the complete Chapter Practice Test

for 13. Achieving Energy Sustainability
on all key terms, persons, places, and concepts.

Online 99 Cents

http://www.epub89.16.23086.13.cram101.com/

Use www.Cram101.com for all your study needs

including Cram101's online interactive problem solving labs in

chemistry, statistics, mathematics, and more.

Visit Cram101.com for full Practice Exams

14. Water Pollution

CHAPTER OUTLINE: KEY TERMS, PEOPLE, PLACES, CONCEPTS

Water pollution

Algal bloom

Wastewater

Biochemical oxygen demand

Cultural eutrophication

Dead zone

Eutrophication

Indicator species

Sludge

Anaerobic lagoon

Heavy metal

Hormone

Carcinogen

Cuyahoga River

Polybrominated diphenyl ethers

Sea otters

Thermal pollution

Thermal shock

Clean Water Act

Noise pollution

Safe Drinking Water Act

Visit Cram101.com for full Practice Exams

14. Water Pollution

CHAPTER HIGHLIGHTS & NOTES: KEY TERMS, PEOPLE, PLACES, CONCEPTS

Water pollution	Water pollution is the contamination of water bodies (e.g. lakes, rivers, oceans, aquifers and groundwater). Water pollution occurs when pollutants are discharged directly or indirectly into water bodies without adequate treatment to remove harmful compounds. Water pollution affects plants and organisms living in these bodies of water.
Algal bloom	An algal bloom is a rapid increase or accumulation in the population of algae in an aquatic system. Algal blooms may occur in freshwater as well as marine environments. Typically, only one or a small number of phytoplankton species are involved, and some blooms may be recognized by discoloration of the water resulting from the high density of pigmented cells.
Wastewater	Wastewater, is any water that has been adversely affected in quality by anthropogenic influence. Municipal wastewater is usually conveyed in a combined sewer or sanitary sewer, and treated at a wastewater treatment plant or septic tank. Treated wastewater is discharged into a receiving water via an effluent sewer.
Biochemical oxygen demand	Biochemical oxygen demand is the amount of dissolved oxygen needed by aerobic biological organisms in a body of water to break down organic material present in a given water sample at certain temperature over a specific time period. The term also refers to a chemical procedure for determining this amount. This is not a precise quantitative test, although it is widely used as an indication of the organic quality of water.
Cultural eutrophication	Cultural eutrophication is the pross that speeds up natural eutrophication because of human activity. Due to clearing of land and building of towns and cities, land runoff is aclerated and more nutrients such as phosphates and nitrate are supplied to lakes and rivers, and then to coastal estuaries and bays. Extra nutrients are also supplied by treatment plants, golf courses, fertilizers, and farms.
Dead zone	Dead zones are hypoxic (low-oxygen) areas in the world's oceans, the observed incidences of which have been increasing since oceanographers began noting them in the 1970s. These occur near inhabited coastlines, where aquatic life is most concentrated. (The vast middle portions of the oceans which naturally have little life are not considered 'dead zones'). The term can also be applied to the identical phenomenon in large lakes.
Eutrophication	Eutrophication or more precisely hypertrophication, is the ecosystem response to the addition of artificial or natural substances, such as nitrates and phosphates, through fertilizers or sewage, to an aquatic system. One example is the 'bloom' or great increase of phytoplankton in a water body as a response to increased levels of nutrients. Negative environmental effects include hypoxia, the depletion of oxygen in the water, which induces reductions in specific fish and other animal populations.

Visit Cram101.com for full Practice Exams

14. Water Pollution

CHAPTER HIGHLIGHTS & NOTES: KEY TERMS, PEOPLE, PLACES, CONCEPTS

Indicator species	An indicator species is any biological species that defines a trait or characteristic of the environment. For example, a species may delineate an ecoregion or indicate an environmental condition such as a disease outbreak, pollution, species competition or climate change. Indicator species can be among the most sensitive species in a region, and sometimes act as an early warning to monitoring biologists.
Sludge	Sludge refers to the residual, semi-solid material left from industrial wastewater, or sewage treatment processes. It can also refer to the settled suspension obtained from conventional drinking water treatment, and numerous other industrial processes. The term is also sometimes used as a generic term for solids separated from suspension in a liquid; this 'soupy' material usually contains significant quantities of 'interstitial' water (between the solid particles).
Anaerobic lagoon	Anaerobic Lagoon is a man-made outdoor earthen basin filled with anim waste that undergoes anaerobic respiration as part of a system designed to manage and treat refuse created by Concentrated Anim Feeding Operations (CAFOs). Anaerobic lagoons are created from a manure slurry, which is washed out from underneath the anim pens and then piped into the lagoon. Sometimes the slurry is placed in an intermediary holding tank under or next to the barns before it is deposited in a lagoon.
Heavy metal	A heavy metal is a member of a loosely-defined subset of elements that exhibit metallic properties. It mainly includes the transition metals, some metalloids, lanthanides, and actinides. Many different definitions have been proposed--some based on density, some on atomic number or atomic weight, and some on chemical properties or toxicity.
Hormone	A hormone is a chemical released by a cell or a gland in one part of the body that sends out messages that affect cells in other parts of the organism. Only a small amount of hormone is required to alter cell metabolism. In essence, it is a chemical messenger that transports a signal from one cell to another.
Carcinogen	A carcinogen is any substance, radionuclide or radiation, that is an agent directly involved in causing cancer. This may be due to the ability to damage the genome or to the disruption of cellular metabolic processes. Several radioactive substances are considered carcinogens, but their carcinogenic activity is attributed to the radiation, for example gamma rays and alpha particles, which they emit.
Cuyahoga River	The Cuyahoga River is located in Northeast Ohio in the United States. Outside of Ohio, the river is most famous for being 'the river that caught fire', helping to spur the environmental movement in the late 1960s. Native Americans called this winding water 'Cuyahoga,' which means 'ooked river' in the Iroquois language.
Polybrominated diphenyl ethers	Polybrominated diphenyl ethers, are organobromine compounds that are used as flame retardants.

Visit Cram101.com for full Practice Exams

14. Water Pollution

CHAPTER HIGHLIGHTS & NOTES: KEY TERMS, PEOPLE, PLACES, CONCEPTS

Like other brominated flame retardants, PBDEs have been used in a wide array of products, including building materials, electronics, furnishings, motor vehicles, airplanes, plastics, polyurethane foams, and textiles. They are structurally akin to the PCBs and other polyhalogenated compounds, consisting of two halogenated aromatic rings.

Sea otters

The sea otter (Enhydra lutris) is a marine mammal native to the coasts of the northern and eastern North Pacific Ocean. Adult sea otters typically weigh between 14 and 45 kg (31 and 99 lb), making them the heaviest members of the weasel family, but among the smallest marine mammals.

Sea otters, whose numbers were once estimated at 150,000-300,000, were hunted extensively for their fur between 1741 and 1911, and the world population fell to 1,000-2,000 individuals living in a fraction of their historic range. A subsequent international ban on hunting, conservation efforts, and reintroduction programs into previously populated areas have contributed to numbers rebounding, and the species now occupies about two-thirds of its former range. The recovery of the sea otter is considered an important success in marine conservation, although populations in the Aleutian Islands and California have recently declined or have plateaued at depressed levels.

Thermal pollution

Thermal pollution is the degradation of water quality by any process that changes ambient water temperature.

A common cause of thermal pollution is the use of water as a coolant by power plants and industrial manufacturers. When water used as a coolant is returned to the natural environment at a higher temperature, the change in temperature decreases oxygen supply, and affects ecosystem composition.

Thermal shock

Thermal shock is the name given to extreme temperature difference (gradient) across an object, which can result in cracking and/or breaking. Glass and ceramic objec are particularly vulnerable to this form of failure, due to their low toughness and low thermal conductivity. However, they are used in many high temperature applications due to their high melting point.

Clean Water Act

The Clean Water Act is the primary federal law in the United States governing water pollution. Commonly abbreviated as the Clean Water Act, the act established the goals of eliminating releases of high amounts of toxic substances into water, eliminating additional water pollution by 1985, and ensuring that surface waters would meet standards necessary for human sports and recreation by 1983.

The principal body of law currently in effect is based on the Federal Water Pollution Control Amendments of 1972 and was significantly expanded from the Federal Water Pollution Control Amendments of 1948. Major amendments were enacted in the Clean Water Act of 1977 and the Water Quality Act of 1987.

Visit Cram101.com for full Practice Exams

14. Water Pollution

125

CHAPTER HIGHLIGHTS & NOTES: KEY TERMS, PEOPLE, PLACES, CONCEPTS

Noise pollution	Noise pollution is excessive, displeasing human, animal, or machine-created environmental noise that disrupts the activity or balance of human or animal life. The word noise may be from the Latin word nauseas, metaphorically meaning disgust or discomfort.
	The source of most outdoor noise worldwide is mainly construction and transportation systems, including motor vehicle noise, aircraft noise, and rail noise.
Safe Drinking Water Act	The Safe Drinking Water Act is the principal federal law in the United States intended to ensure safe drinking water for the public. Pursuant to the act, the Environmental Protection Agency (EPA) is required to set standards for drinking water quality and oversee all states, localities, and water suppliers who implement these standards.
	Safe Drinking Water Act applies to every public water system in the United States.

CHAPTER QUIZ: KEY TERMS, PEOPLE, PLACES, CONCEPTS

1. _____ or more precisely hypertrophication, is the ecosystem response to the addition of artificial or natural substances, such as nitrates and phosphates, through fertilizers or sewage, to an aquatic system. One example is the 'bloom' or great increase of phytoplankton in a water body as a response to increased levels of nutrients. Negative environmental effects include hypoxia, the depletion of oxygen in the water, which induces reductions in specific fish and other animal populations.

   a. Ice algae
   b. Eutrophication
   c. Igap
   d. Interflow

2. _____, is any water that has been adversely affected in quality by anthropogenic influence. Municipal _____ is usually conveyed in a combined sewer or sanitary sewer, and treated at a _____ treatment plant or septic tank. Treated _____ is discharged into a receiving water via an effluent sewer.

   a. Wastewater
   b. Water balance
   c. Water pollution
   d. Water resource policy

3. . An _____ is a rapid increase or accumulation in the population of algae in an aquatic system. _____s may occur in freshwater as well as marine environments. Typically, only one or a small number of phytoplankton species are involved, and some blooms may be recognized by discoloration of the water resulting from the high density of pigmented cells.

Visit Cram101.com for full Practice Exams

14. Water Pollution

CHAPTER QUIZ: KEY TERMS, PEOPLE, PLACES, CONCEPTS

    a. Algal bloom

    b. Index of biological integrity

    c. Odyssey

    d. Whale fall

4. A _____ is a member of a loosely-defined subset of elements that exhibit metallic properties. It mainly includes the transition metals, some metalloids, lanthanides, and actinides. Many different definitions have been proposed-- some based on density, some on atomic number or atomic weight, and some on chemical properties or toxicity.

    a. Heavy metal

    b. High Production Volume Chemicals Programme

    c. Kombucha

    d. Maximum tolerated dose

5. The _____ is the primary federal law in the United States governing water pollution. Commonly abbreviated as the _____, the act established the goals of eliminating releases of high amounts of toxic substances into water, eliminating additional water pollution by 1985, and ensuring that surface waters would meet standards necessary for human sports and recreation by 1983.

The principal body of law currently in effect is based on the Federal Water Pollution Control Amendments of 1972 and was significantly expanded from the Federal Water Pollution Control Amendments of 1948. Major amendments were enacted in the _____ of 1977 and the Water Quality Act of 1987.

    a. Federal Insecticide, Fungicide, and Rodenticide Act

    b. Clean Water Act

    c. Gibbons v. Ogden

    d. Wastewater

Visit Cram101.com for full Practice Exams

Visit Cram101.com for full Practice Exams

ANSWER KEY
14. Water Pollution

1. b
2. a
3. a
4. a
5. b

You can take the complete Chapter Practice Test

for 14. Water Pollution
on all key terms, persons, places, and concepts.

Online 99 Cents

http://www.epub89.16.23086.14.cram101.com/

Use www.Cram101.com for all your study needs

including Cram101's online interactive problem solving labs in

chemistry, statistics, mathematics, and more.

Visit Cram101.com for full Practice Exams

15. Air Pollution and Stratospheric Ozone Depletion

CHAPTER OUTLINE: KEY TERMS, PEOPLE, PLACES, CONCEPTS

_____ Air pollution _____

_____ Clean Air Act _____

_____ Particulate matter _____

_____ Smog _____

_____ Bioaccumulation _____

_____ Great Smoky Mountains _____

_____ Formation _____

_____ Electrostatic precipitator _____

_____ Scrubber _____

_____ Ozone layer _____

_____ Montreal Protocol _____

CHAPTER HIGHLIGHTS & NOTES: KEY TERMS, PEOPLE, PLACES, CONCEPTS

Air pollution	Air pollution is the introduction into the atmosphere of chemicals, particulates, or biological materials that cause discomfort, disease, or death to humans, damage other living organisms such as food crops, or damage the natural environment or built environment. The atmosphere is a complex dynamic natural gaseous system that is essential to support life on planet Earth. Stratospheric ozone depletion due to air pollution has long been recognized as a threat to human health as well as to the Earth's ecosystems.
Clean Air Act	The Clean Air Act is a United States federal law designed to control air pollution on a national level. It requires the Environmental Protection Agency (EPA) to develop and enforce regulations to protect the public from airborne contaminants known to be hazardous to human health. The 1963 version of the legislation established a research program, expanded in 1967.

Visit Cram101.com for full Practice Exams

15. Air Pollution and Stratospheric Ozone Depletion

CHAPTER HIGHLIGHTS & NOTES: KEY TERMS, PEOPLE, PLACES, CONCEPTS

Particulate matter	Atmospheric particulate matter - also known as particulates or particulate matter - are tiny pieces of solid or liquid matter associated with the Earth's atmosphere. They are suspended in the atmosphere as atmospheric aerosol, a term which refers to the particulate/air mixture, as opposed to the particulate matter alone. However, it is common to use the term aerosol to refer to the particulate component alone.
Smog	Smog is a type of air pollution; the word 'smog' was coined in the early 20th century as a portmanteau of the words smoke and fog to refer to smoky fog. The word was then intended to refer to what was sometimes known as pea soup fog, a familiar and serious problem in London from the 19th century to the mid 20th century. This kind of smog is caused by the burning of large amounts of coal within a city; this smog contains soot particulates from smoke, sulfur dioxide and other components.
Bioaccumulation	Bioaccumulation refers to the accumulation of substances, such as pesticides, or other organic chemicals in an organism. Bioaccumulation occurs when an organism absorbs a toxic substance at a rate greater than that at which the substance is lost. Thus, the longer the biological half-life of the substance the greater the risk of chronic poisoning, even if environmental levels of the toxin are not very high.
Great Smoky Mountains	The Great Smoky Mountains are a mountain range rising along the Tennessee-North Carolina border in the southeastern United States. They are a subrange of the Appalachian Mountains, and form part of the Blue Ridge Physiographic Province. The range is sometimes called the Smoky or Smokey Mountains, and the name is commonly shortened to the Smokies.
Formation	A formation is the fundamental unit of lithostratigraphy. A formation consists of a certain number of rock strata that have a comparable lithology, facies or other similar properties. Formations are not defined on the thickness of the rock strata they consist of and the thickness of different formations can therefore vary widely.
Electrostatic precipitator	An electrostatic precipitator or electrostatic air cleaner is a particulate collection device that removes particles from a flowing gas (such as air) using the force of an induced electrostatic charge. Electrostatic precipitators are highly efficient filtration devices that minimally impede the flow of gases through the device, and can easily remove fine particulate matter such as dust and smoke from the air stream. In contrast to wet scrubbers which apply energy directly to the flowing fluid medium, an ESP applies energy only to the particulate matter being collected and therefore is very efficient in its consumption of energy (in the form of electricity).
Scrubber	'Scrubber' systems are a diverse group of air pollution control devices that can be used to remove some particulates and/or gases from industrial exhaust streams. Traditionally, the term 'scrubber' has referred to pollution control devices that use liquid to wash unwanted pollutants from a gas stream.

Visit Cram101.com for full Practice Exams

15. Air Pollution and Stratospheric Ozone Depletion

CHAPTER HIGHLIGHTS & NOTES: KEY TERMS, PEOPLE, PLACES, CONCEPTS

Ozone layer	The ozone layer is a layer in Earth's atmosphere which contains relatively high concentrations of ozone (O_3). This layer absorbs 97-99% of the Sun's high frequency ultraviet light, which potentially damages the life forms on Earth. It is mainly located in the lower portion of the stratosphere from approximately 20 to 30 kilometres (12 to 19 mi) above Earth, though the thickness varies seasonally and geographically.
Montreal Protocol	The Montreal Protocol on Substances That Deplete the Ozone Layer (a protocol to the Vienna Convention for the Protection of the Ozone Layer) is an international treaty designed to protect the ozone layer by phasing out the production of numerous substances believed to be responsible for ozone depletion. The treaty was opened for signature on September 16, 1987, and entered into force on January 1, 1989, followed by a first meeting in Helsinki, May 1989. Since then, it has undergone seven revisions, in 1990 (London), 1991 (Nairobi), 1992 (Copenhagen), 1993 (Bangkok), 1995 (Vienna), 1997 (Montreal), and 1999 (Beijing). It is believed that if the international agreement is adhered to, the ozone layer is expected to recover by 2050. Due to its widespread adoption and implementation it has been hailed as an example of exceptional international co-operation, with Kofi Annan quoted as saying that 'perhaps the single most successful international agreement to date has been the Montreal Protocol'.

CHAPTER QUIZ: KEY TERMS, PEOPLE, PLACES, CONCEPTS

1. _____ is a type of air pollution; the word '_____' was coined in the early 20th century as a portmanteau of the words smoke and fog to refer to smoky fog. The word was then intended to refer to what was sometimes known as pea soup fog, a familiar and serious problem in London from the 19th century to the mid 20th century. This kind of _____ is caused by the burning of large amounts of coal within a city; this _____ contains soot particulates from smoke, sulfur dioxide and other components.

   a. Summer smog
   b. particulate matter
   c. Juglone
   d. Smog

2. . _____ is the introduction into the atmosphere of chemicals, particulates, or biological materials that cause discomfort, disease, or death to humans, damage other living organisms such as food crops, or damage the natural environment or built environment.

   The atmosphere is a complex dynamic natural gaseous system that is essential to support life on planet Earth. Stratospheric ozone depletion due to _____ has long been recognized as a threat to human health as well as to the Earth's ecosystems.

   a. Air pollution

Visit Cram101.com for full Practice Exams

15. Air Pollution and Stratospheric Ozone Depletion

CHAPTER QUIZ: KEY TERMS, PEOPLE, PLACES, CONCEPTS

b. Aerotoxic syndrome

c. Air Quality Health Index

d. Air quality index

3. A _____ is the fundamental unit of lithostratigraphy. A _____ consists of a certain number of rock strata that have a comparable lithology, facies or other similar properties. _____s are not defined on the thickness of the rock strata they consist of and the thickness of different _____s can therefore vary widely.

a. Tamala limestone

b. Formation

c. Juglone

d. King Range Wilderness

4. The _____ is a United States federal law designed to control air pollution on a national level. It requires the Environmental Protection Agency (EPA) to develop and enforce regulations to protect the public from airborne contaminants known to be hazardous to human health. The 1963 version of the legislation established a research program, expanded in 1967. Major amendments to the law, requiring regulatory controls for air pollution, passed in 1970, 1977 and 1990.

a. fragmentation

b. cultivation

c. Leopold

d. Clean Air Act

5. An _____ or electrostatic air cleaner is a particulate collection device that removes particles from a flowing gas (such as air) using the force of an induced electrostatic charge. _____s are highly efficient filtration devices that minimally impede the flow of gases through the device, and can easily remove fine particulate matter such as dust and smoke from the air stream. In contrast to wet scrubbers which apply energy directly to the flowing fluid medium, an ESP applies energy only to the particulate matter being collected and therefore is very efficient in its consumption of energy (in the form of electricity).

a. Emission test cycle

b. Electrostatic precipitator

c. In situ chemical oxidation

d. In situ chemical reduction

Visit Cram101.com for full Practice Exams

Visit Cram101.com for full Practice Exams

ANSWER KEY
15. Air Pollution and Stratospheric Ozone Depletion

1. d
2. a
3. b
4. d
5. b

You can take the complete Chapter Practice Test

for 15. Air Pollution and Stratospheric Ozone Depletion
on all key terms, persons, places, and concepts.

Online 99 Cents

http://www.epub89.16.23086.15.cram101.com/

Use www.Cram101.com for all your study needs

including Cram101's online interactive problem solving labs in

chemistry, statistics, mathematics, and more.

Visit Cram101.com for full Practice Exams

16. Waste Generation and Waste Disposal

CHAPTER OUTLINE: KEY TERMS, PEOPLE, PLACES, CONCEPTS

	Polystyrene
	Detritivore
	Planned obsolescence
	E-waste
	Source reduction
	Leachate
	Environmental justice
	Water pollution
	Bottom ash
	Fly ash
	Hazardous waste
	National Priorities List
	Love Canal
	Life-cycle assessment
	Michael Braungart

Visit Cram101.com for full Practice Exams

16. Waste Generation and Waste Disposal

CHAPTER HIGHLIGHTS & NOTES: KEY TERMS, PEOPLE, PLACES, CONCEPTS

Polystyrene	Polystyrene is an aromatic polymer made from the monomer styrene, a liquid hydrocarbon that is manufactured from petroleum by the chemical industry. Polystyrene is one of the most widely used plastics, the scale being several billion kilograms per year.
	Polystyrene is a thermoplastic substance, which is in solid (glassy) state at room temperature, but flows if heated above its glass transition temperature of about 100 °C (for molding or extrusion), and becomes solid again when cooled.
Detritivore	Detritivores, also known as detritophages or detritus feeders or detritus eaters or saprophages, are heterotrophs that obtain nutrients by consuming detritus (decomposing organic matter). By doing so, they contribute to decomposition and the nutrient cycles. They should be distinguished from other decomposers, such as many species of bacteria, fungi and protists, unable to ingest discrete lumps of matter, instead live by absorbing and metabolising on a molecular scale.
Planned obsolescence	Planned obsolescence is a licy of planning or designing a product with a limited useful life, so it will become obsolete, that is, unfashionable or no longer functional after a certain period of time. Planned obsolescence has tential benefits for a producer because to obtain continuing use of the product the consumer is under pressure to purchase again, whether from the same manufacturer (a replacement part or a newer model), or from a competitor which might also rely on planned obsolescence.
	In some cases, deliberate deprecation of earlier versions of a technology is used to reduce ongoing suprt costs, especially in the software industry.
E-waste	E-waste, e-scrap, or waste electrical and electronic equipment (WEEE) describes discarded electrical or electronic devices. There is a lack of consensus as to whether the term should apply to resale, reuse, and refurbishing industries, or only to product that cannot be used for its intended purpose. Informal processing of electronic waste in developing countries may cause serious health and pollution problems, though these countries are also most likely to reuse and repair electronics.
Source reduction	Source reduction refers to any change in the design, manufacture, purchase, or use of materials or products (including packaging) to reduce their amount or toxicity before they become municipal solid waste.
	Synonyms
	Pollution Prevention (or P2) and Toxics use reduction are also called source reduction because they address the use of hazardous substances at the source.
	Procedures

Visit Cram101.com for full Practice Exams

16. Waste Generation and Waste Disposal

CHAPTER HIGHLIGHTS & NOTES: KEY TERMS, PEOPLE, PLACES, CONCEPTS

Leachate	Leachate is any liquid that, in passing through matter, extracts solutes, suspended solids or any other component of the material through which it has passed. Leachate is a widely used term in the environmental sciences where it has the specific meaning of a liquid that has dissolved or entrained environmentally harmful substances which may then enter the environment. It is most commonly used in the context of land-filling of putrescible or industrial waste.
Environmental justice	The term environmental justice emerged as a concept in the United States in the early 1980s. The term has two distinct uses. The first and more common usage describes a social movement in the United States whose focus is on the fair distribution of environmental benefits and burdens.
Water pollution	Water pollution is the contamination of water bodies (e.g. lakes, rivers, oceans, aquifers and groundwater). Water pollution occurs when pollutants are discharged directly or indirectly into water bodies without adequate treatment to remove harmful compounds. Water pollution affects plants and organisms living in these bodies of water.
Bottom ash	Bottom ash refers to part of the non-combustible residues of combustion. In an industrial context, it usually refers to coal combustion and comprises traces of combustibles embedded in forming clinkers and sticking to hot side walls of a coal-burning furnace during its operation. The portion of the ash that escapes up the chimney or stack is, however, referred to as fly ash.
Fly ash	Fly ash is one of the residues generated in combustion, and comprises the fine particles that rise with the flue gases. Ash which does not rise is termed bottom ash. In an industrial context, fly ash usually refers to ash produced during combustion of coal.
Hazardous waste	A Hazardous waste is waste that poses substantial or potential threats to public health or the environment. In the United States, the treatment, storage and disposal of hazardous waste is regulated under the Resource Conservation and Recovery Act (RCRA). Hazardous wastes are defined under RCRA in 40 CFR 261 where they are divided into two major categories: characteristic wastes and listed wastes.
National Priorities List	The National Priorities List is the list of hazardous waste sites in the United States eligible for long-term remedial action (cleanup) financed under the federal Superfund program. Environmental Protection Agency (EPA) regulations outline a formal process for assessing hazardous waste sites and placing them on the . The is intended primarily to guide EPA in determining which sites warrant further investigation. The inclusion of a facility in the National Priorities List does not reflect a judgment of its owner or operator or make the owner or operator take any action.

Visit Cram101.com for full Practice Exams

16. Waste Generation and Waste Disposal

CHAPTER HIGHLIGHTS & NOTES: KEY TERMS, PEOPLE, PLACES, CONCEPTS

Love Canal	Love Canal was a neighborhood in Niagara Falls, New York, located in the white collar LaSalle section of the city. It officially covers 36 square blocks in the far southeastern corner of the city, along 99th Street and Read Avenue. Two bodies of water define the northern and southern boundaries of the neighborhood: Bergholtz Creek to the north and the Niagara River one-quarter mile (400 m) to the south.
Life-cycle assessment	A life-cycle assessment is a technique to assess environmental impacts associated with all the stages of a product's life from-cradle-to-grave (i.e., from raw material extraction through materials processing, manufacture, distribution, use, repair and maintenance, and disposal or recycling). 's can help avoid a narrow outlook on environmental concerns by:•Compiling an inventory of relevant energy and material inputs and environmental releases;•Evaluating the potential impacts associated with identified inputs and releases;•Interpreting the results to help you make a more informed decision.Goals and purpose

The goal of is to compare the full range of environmental effects assignable to products and services in order to improve processes, support policy and provide a sound basis for informed decisions.

The term life cycle refers to the notion that a fair, holistic assessment requires the assessment of raw-material production, manufacture, distribution, use and disposal including all intervening transportation steps necessary or caused by the product's existence. |
| Michael Braungart | |

CHAPTER QUIZ: KEY TERMS, PEOPLE, PLACES, CONCEPTS

1. _____ is an aromatic polymer made from the monomer styrene, a liquid hydrocarbon that is manufactured from petroleum by the chemical industry. _____ is one of the most widely used plastics, the scale being several billion kilograms per year.

   _____ is a thermoplastic substance, which is in solid (glassy) state at room temperature, but flows if heated above its glass transition temperature of about 100 °C (for molding or extrusion), and becomes solid again when cooled.

   a. Polyvinyl chloride
   b. Polystyrene
   c. Gibbons v. Ogden
   d. Krakatoa

2. . _____s, also known as detritophages or detritus feeders or detritus eaters or saprophages, are heterotrophs that obtain nutrients by consuming detritus (decomposing organic matter). By doing so, they contribute to decomposition and the nutrient cycles.

Visit Cram101.com for full Practice Exams

16. Waste Generation and Waste Disposal

139

CHAPTER QUIZ: KEY TERMS, PEOPLE, PLACES, CONCEPTS

They should be distinguished from other decomposers, such as many species of bacteria, fungi and protists, unable to ingest discrete lumps of matter, instead live by absorbing and metabolising on a molecular scale.

a. nitrification
b. Juglone
c. Detritivore
d. Krakatoa

3. _____ refers to part of the non-combustible residues of combustion. In an industrial context, it usually refers to coal combustion and comprises traces of combustibles embedded in forming clinkers and sticking to hot side walls of a coal-burning furnace during its operation. The portion of the ash that escapes up the chimney or stack is, however, referred to as fly ash.

a. Bulky waste
b. Chaff
c. Chat
d. Bottom ash

4. _____ is a licy of planning or designing a product with a limited useful life, so it will become obsolete, that is, unfashionable or no longer functional after a certain period of time. _____ has tential benefits for a producer because to obtain continuing use of the product the consumer is under pressure to purchase again, whether from the same manufacturer (a replacement part or a newer model), or from a competitor which might also rely on _____.

In some cases, deliberate deprecation of earlier versions of a technology is used to reduce ongoing suprt costs, especially in the software industry.

a. Post-consumer waste
b. Red mud
c. Planned obsolescence
d. Sawdust

5. _____, e-scrap, or waste electrical and electronic equipment (WEEE) describes discarded electrical or electronic devices. There is a lack of consensus as to whether the term should apply to resale, reuse, and refurbishing industries, or only to product that cannot be used for its intended purpose. Informal processing of electronic waste in developing countries may cause serious health and pollution problems, though these countries are also most likely to reuse and repair electronics.

a. Odyssey
b. Red mud
c. E-waste
d. Sawdust

Visit Cram101.com for full Practice Exams

Visit Cram101.com for full Practice Exams

ANSWER KEY
16. Waste Generation and Waste Disposal

1. b
2. c
3. d
4. c
5. c

You can take the complete Chapter Practice Test

for 16. Waste Generation and Waste Disposal
on all key terms, persons, places, and concepts.

Online 99 Cents

http://www.epub89.16.23086.16.cram101.com/

Use www.Cram101.com for all your study needs

including Cram101's online interactive problem solving labs in

chemistry, statistics, mathematics, and more.

Visit Cram101.com for full Practice Exams

17. Human Health and Environmental Risks

CHAPTER OUTLINE: KEY TERMS, PEOPLE, PLACES, CONCEPTS

Infectious diseases

Transmission

Malaria

Tuberculosis

Toxicology

Carcinogen

Allergen

Endocrine disruptor

Hormone

Water pollution

Toxin

Epidemiology

Bioaccumulation

Biomagnification

Environmental hazard

Risk assessment

Asbestosis

Visit Cram101.com for full Practice Exams

17. Human Health and Environmental Risks

143

CHAPTER HIGHLIGHTS & NOTES: KEY TERMS, PEOPLE, PLACES, CONCEPTS

Infectious diseases	Infectious diseases, comprise clinically evident illness (i.e. transmissible diseases or communicable diseases comprise clinically evident illness (i.e. characteristic medical signs and/or symptoms of disease) resulting from the infection, presence and growth of pathogenic biological agents in an individual host organism. In certain cases, infectious diseases may be asymptomatic for much or even all of their course in a given host. In the latter case, the disease may only be defined as a 'disease' (which by definition means an illness) in hosts who secondarily become ill after contact with an asymptomatic carrier.
Transmission	A machine consists of a power source and a power transmission system, which provides controlled application of the power. Merriam-Webster defines transmission as: an assembly of parts including the speed-changing gears and the propeller shaft by which the power is transmitted from an engine to a live axle. Often transmission refers simply to the gearbox that uses gears and gear trains to provide speed and torque conversions from a rotating power source to another device.
Malaria	Malaria is a mosquito-borne infectious disease of humans and other animals caused by protists (a type of microorganism) of the genus Plasmodium. It begins with a bite from an infected female mosquito (Anopheles Mosquito), which introduces the protists via its saliva into the circulatory system, and ultimately to the liver where they mature and reproduce. The disease causes symptoms that typically include fever and headache, which in severe cases can progress to coma or death.
Tuberculosis	Tuberculosis, MTB, or TB is a common, and in many cases lethal, infectious disease caused by various strains of mycobacteria, usually Mycobacterium tuberculosis. Tuberculosis typically attacks the lungs, but can also affect other parts of the body.
Toxicology	Toxicology is a branch of biology, chemistry, and medicine concerned with the study of the adverse effects of chemicals on living organisms. It is the study of symptoms, mechanisms, treatments and detection of poisoning, especially the poisoning of people. Dioscorides, a Greek physician in the court of the Roman emperor Nero, made the first attempt to classify plants according to their toxic and therapeutic effect.
Carcinogen	A carcinogen is any substance, radionuclide or radiation, that is an agent directly involved in causing cancer. This may be due to the ability to damage the genome or to the disruption of cellular metabolic processes. Several radioactive substances are considered carcinogens, but their carcinogenic activity is attributed to the radiation, for example gamma rays and alpha particles, which they emit.
Allergen	An allergen is any substance that can cause an allergy. Technically, an allergen is a non-parasitic antigen capable of stimulating a type-I hypersensitivity reaction in atopic individuals.

Visit Cram101.com for full Practice Exams

17. Human Health and Environmental Risks

CHAPTER HIGHLIGHTS & NOTES: KEY TERMS, PEOPLE, PLACES, CONCEPTS

Endocrine disruptor	Endocrine disruptors are chemicals that interfere with endocrine (or hormone system) in animals, including humans. These disruptions can cause cancerous tumors, birth defects, and other developmental disorders. Specifically, they are known to cause learning disabilities, severe attention deficit disorder, cognitive and brain development problems, deformations of the body (including limbs); sexual development problems, feminizing of males or masculine effects on females, etc.
Hormone	A hormone is a chemical released by a cell or a gland in one part of the body that sends out messages that affect cells in other parts of the organism. Only a small amount of hormone is required to alter cell metabolism. In essence, it is a chemical messenger that transports a signal from one cell to another.
Water pollution	Water pollution is the contamination of water bodies (e.g. lakes, rivers, oceans, aquifers and groundwater). Water pollution occurs when pollutants are discharged directly or indirectly into water bodies without adequate treatment to remove harmful compounds. Water pollution affects plants and organisms living in these bodies of water.
Toxin	A toxin is a poisonous substance produced by living cells or organisms (technically, although humans are living organisms, man-made substances created by artificial processes usually are not considered toxins by this definition). It was the organic chemist Ludwig Brieger (1849-1919) who first used the term 'toxin'. For a toxic substance not produced by living organisms, 'toxicant' is the more appropriate term, and 'toxics' is an acceptable plural.
Epidemiology	Epidemiology is the study of the distribution and patterns of health-events, health-characteristics and their causes or influences in well-defined populations. It is the cornerstone method of public health research, and helps inform policy decisions and evidence-based medicine by identifying risk factors for disease and targets for preventive medicine. Epidemiologists are involved in the design of studies, collection and statistical analysis of data, and interpretation and dissemination of results (including peer review and occasional systematic review).
Bioaccumulation	Bioaccumulation refers to the accumulation of substances, such as pesticides, or other organic chemicals in an organism. Bioaccumulation occurs when an organism absorbs a toxic substance at a rate greater than that at which the substance is lost. Thus, the longer the biological half-life of the substance the greater the risk of chronic poisoning, even if environmental levels of the toxin are not very high.

Visit Cram101.com for full Practice Exams

17. Human Health and Environmental Risks

145

CHAPTER HIGHLIGHTS & NOTES: KEY TERMS, PEOPLE, PLACES, CONCEPTS

Biomagnification	Biomagnification, is the increase in concentration of a substance that occurs in a food chain as a consequence of:•Persistence (can't be broken down by environmental processes)•Food chain energetics•Low (or nonexistent) rate of internal degradation/excretion of the substance (often due to water-insolubility) The following is an example showing how biomagnification takes place in nature: An anchovy eats zooplankton that have tiny amounts of mercury that the zooplankton has picked up from the water throughout the anchovie's lifespan. A tuna eats many of these anchovies over its life, accumulating the mercury in each of those anchovies into its body. If the mercury stunts the growth of the anchovies, that tuna is required to eat more little fish to stay alive.
Environmental hazard	'Environmental hazard' is the state of events which has the potential to threaten the surrounding natural environment and adversely affect people's health. This term incorporates topics like pollution and natural disasters such as storms and earthquakes. Hazards can be categorized in five types:•Chemical•Physical•Mechanical•Biological•Psychosocial Examples•Allergens•Anthrax•Antibiotic agents in animals destined for human consumption•Arbovirus•Arsenic - a contaminant of fresh water sources (water wells)•Asbestos - carcinogenic•Avian influenza•Bovine spongiform encephalopathy (BSE)•Carcinogens•Cholera•Cosmic rays•DDT•dioxins•Drought•Dysentery•Electromagnetic fields•Endocrine disruptors•Epidemics•E-waste•Explosive material•Floods•Food poisoning•Fungicides•Furans•Haloalkanes•Heavy metals•Herbicides•Hormones in animals destined for human consumption•Lead in paint•Light pollution•Lighting•Lightning•Malaria•Marine debris•mercury•Molds•Mutagens•Noise pollution•Onchocerciasis (river blindness)•Pandemics•Pathogens•Pesticides•Pollen for allergic people•Polychlorinated biphenyls•Quicksand•Rabies•Radon and other natural sources of radioactivity•Severe acute respiratory syndrome (SARS)•Sick building syndrome•Soil pollution•Tobacco smoking•Toxic waste•Ultraviolet light•vibration•Wildfire•X-rays .
Risk assessment	Risk assessment is a step in a risk management procedure. Risk assessment is the determination of quantitative or qualitative value of risk related to a concrete situation and a recognized threat (also called hazard). Quantitative risk assessment requires calculations of two components of risk (R):, the magnitude of the potential loss (L), and the probability (p) that the loss will occur.
Asbestosis	Asbestosis is a chronic inflammatory and fibrotic medical condition affecting the parenchymal tissue of the lungs caused by the inhalation and retention of asbestos fibers. It usually occurs after high intensity and/or long-term exposure to asbestos (particularly in those individuals working on the production or end-use of products containing asbestos) and is therefore regarded as an occupational lung disease. People with extensive occupational exposure to the mining, manufacturing, handling, or removal of asbestos are at risk of developing asbestosis.

Visit Cram101.com for full Practice Exams

17. Human Health and Environmental Risks

CHAPTER QUIZ: KEY TERMS, PEOPLE, PLACES, CONCEPTS

1. '_____' is the state of events which has the potential to threaten the surrounding natural environment and adversely affect people's health. This term incorporates topics like pollution and natural disasters such as storms and earthquakes. Hazards can be categorized in five types:•Chemical•Physical•Mechanical•Biological•Psychosocial Examples•Allergens•Anthrax•Antibiotic agents in animals destined for human consumption•Arbovirus•Arsenic - a contaminant of fresh water sources (water wells)•Asbestos - carcinogenic•Avian influenza•Bovine spongiform encephalopathy (BSE)•Carcinogens•Cholera•Cosmic rays•DDT•dioxins•Drought•Dysentery•Electromagnetic fields•Endocrine disruptors•Epidemics•E-waste•Explosive material•Floods•Food poisoning•Fungicides•Furans•Haloalkanes•Heavy metals•Herbicides•Hormones in animals destined for human consumption•Lead in paint•Light pollution•Lighting•Lightning•Malaria•Marine debris•mercury•Molds•Mutagens•Noise pollution•Onchocerciasis (river blindness)•Pandemics•Pathogens•Pesticides•Pollen for allergic people•Polychlorinated biphenyls•Quicksand•Rabies•Radon and other natural sources of radioactivity•Severe acute respiratory syndrome (SARS)•Sick building syndrome•Soil pollution•Tobacco smoking•Toxic waste•Ultraviolet light•vibration•Wildfire•X-rays .

   a. Environmental health officer
   b. Environmental medicine
   c. Exposure science
   d. Environmental hazard

2. _____ is a branch of biology, chemistry, and medicine concerned with the study of the adverse effects of chemicals on living organisms. It is the study of symptoms, mechanisms, treatments and detection of poisoning, especially the poisoning of people.

   Dioscorides, a Greek physician in the court of the Roman emperor Nero, made the first attempt to classify plants according to their toxic and therapeutic effect.

   a. Alfonso Jordan
   b. Toxicology
   c. Rowland Hill
   d. Richard Russell Waldron

3. A _____ is any substance, radionuclide or radiation, that is an agent directly involved in causing cancer. This may be due to the ability to damage the genome or to the disruption of cellular metabolic processes. Several radioactive substances are considered _____s, but their carcinogenic activity is attributed to the radiation, for example gamma rays and alpha particles, which they emit.

   a. Juglone
   b. Gibbons v. Ogden
   c. Krakatoa
   d. Carcinogen

4. . _____ is a mosquito-borne infectious disease of humans and other animals caused by protists (a type of microorganism) of the genus Plasmodium. It begins with a bite from an infected female mosquito (Anopheles Mosquito), which introduces the protists via its saliva into the circulatory system, and ultimately to the liver where they mature and reproduce.

Visit Cram101.com for full Practice Exams

17. Human Health and Environmental Risks

CHAPTER QUIZ: KEY TERMS, PEOPLE, PLACES, CONCEPTS

The disease causes symptoms that typically include fever and headache, which in severe cases can progress to coma or death.

a. Malaria
b. Gibbons v. Ogden
c. Krakatoa
d. Diesel engine

5. _____ is a chronic inflammatory and fibrotic medical condition affecting the parenchymal tissue of the lungs caused by the inhalation and retention of asbestos fibers. It usually occurs after high intensity and/or long-term exposure to asbestos (particularly in those individuals working on the production or end-use of products containing asbestos) and is therefore regarded as an occupational lung disease. People with extensive occupational exposure to the mining, manufacturing, handling, or removal of asbestos are at risk of developing _____.

a. Juglone
b. Asbestosis
c. Exposure science
d. Intake fraction

Visit Cram101.com for full Practice Exams

Visit Cram101.com for full Practice Exams

ANSWER KEY
17. Human Health and Environmental Risks

1. d
2. b
3. d
4. a
5. b

You can take the complete Chapter Practice Test

for 17. Human Health and Environmental Risks
on all key terms, persons, places, and concepts.

Online 99 Cents

http://www.epub89.16.23086.17.cram101.com/

Use www.Cram101.com for all your study needs

including Cram101's online interactive problem solving labs in

chemistry, statistics, mathematics, and more.

Visit Cram101.com for full Practice Exams

18. Conservation of Biodiversity

CHAPTER OUTLINE: KEY TERMS, PEOPLE, PLACES, CONCEPTS

Polar

Charles Darwin

Extinction

Inbreeding depression

Biodiversity hotspot

Millennium Ecosystem Assessment

Global change

Invasive species

Dodo

Overexploitation

Sea otters

Endangered Species Act

Ecosystem

Island biogeography

Biosphere reserves

Habitat corridor

Debt-for-nature swap

Visit Cram101.com for full Practice Exams

18. Conservation of Biodiversity

CHAPTER HIGHLIGHTS & NOTES: KEY TERMS, PEOPLE, PLACES, CONCEPTS

Polar	The Global Geospace Science (GGS) Polar Satellite was a NASA science spacecraft designed to study the polar magnetosphere and aurora. It was launched into orbit in February 1996, and continued operations until the program was terminated in April 2008. The spacecraft remains in orbit, though it is now inactive. Polar is the sister ship to GGS Wind.
Charles Darwin	Charles Darwin, FRS (12 February 1809 - 19 April 1882) was an English naturalist. He established that all species of life have descended over time from common ancestors, and proposed the scientific theory that this branching pattern of evolution resulted from a process that he called natural selection, in which the struggle for existence has a similar effect to the artificial selection involved in selective breeding.
	Charles Darwin published his theory of evolution with compelling evidence in his 1859 book On the Origin of Species, overcoming scientific rejection of earlier concepts of transmutation of species.
Extinction	In biology and ecology, extinction is the end of an organism or of a group of organisms (taxon), normally a species. The moment of extinction is generally considered to be the death of the last individual of the species, although the capacity to breed and recover may have been lost before this point. Because a species' potential range may be very large, determining this moment is difficult, and is usually done retrospectively.
Inbreeding depression	Inbreeding depression is the reduced fitness in a given population as a result of breeding of related individuals. It is often the result of a population bottleneck. In general, the higher the genetic variation within a breeding population, the less likely it is to suffer from inbreeding depression.
Biodiversity hotspot	A biodiversity hotspot is a biogeographic region with a significant reservoir of biodiversity that is under threat from humans.
	The concept of biodiversity hotspots was originated by Norman Myers in two articles in 'The Environmentalist' (1988), & 1990 revised after thorough analysis by Myers and others in 'Hotspots: Earth's Biologically Richest and Most Endangered Terrestrial Ecoregions'.
	To qualify as a biodiversity hotspot on Myers 2000 edition of the hotspot-map, a region must meet two strict criteria: it must contain at least 0.5% or 1,500 species of vascular plants as endemics, and it has to have lost at least 70% of its primary vegetation.
Millennium Ecosystem Assessment	The Millennium Ecosystem Assessment, released in 2005, is an international synthesis by over 1000 of the world's leading biological scientists that analyzes the state of the Earth's ecosystems and provides summaries and guidelines for decision-makers. It concludes that human activity is having a significant and escalating impact on the biodiversity of world ecosystems, reducing both their resilience and biocapacity. The report refers to natural systems as humanity's 'life-support system', providing essential 'ecosystem services'.

Visit Cram101.com for full Practice Exams

18. Conservation of Biodiversity

CHAPTER HIGHLIGHTS & NOTES: KEY TERMS, PEOPLE, PLACES, CONCEPTS

Global change	Global change refers to planetary-scale changes in the Earth system. The system consists of the land, oceans, atmosphere, poles, life, the planet's natural cycles and deep Earth processes. These constituent parts influence one another.
Invasive species	Invasive species, is a nomenclature term and categorization phrase used for flora and fauna, and for specific restoration-preservation processes in native habitats, with several definitions:•The first definition, the most used, applies to introduced species (also called 'non-indigenous' or 'non-native') that adversely affect the habitats and bioregions they invade economically, environmentally, and/or ecologically. Such invasive species may be either plants or animals and may disrupt by dominating a region, wilderness areas, particular habitats, or wildland-urban interface land from loss of natural controls (such as predators or herbivores). This includes non-native invasive plant species labeled as exotic pest plants and invasive exotics growing in native plant communities.
Dodo	The dodo was a flightless bird endemic to the Indian Ocean island of Mauritius. It stood about a metre (3.3 feet) tall, weighing about 20 kilograms (44 lb). The dodo lost the power of flight because food was abundant and mammalian predators were absent on Mauritius.
Overexploitation	Overexploitation, refers to harvesting a renewable resource to the point of diminishing returns. Sustained overexploitation can lead to the destruction of the resource. The term applies to natural resources such as: wild medicinal plants, grazing pastures, fish stocks, forests and water aquifers.
Sea otters	The sea otter (Enhydra lutris) is a marine mammal native to the coasts of the northern and eastern North Pacific Ocean. Adult sea otters typically weigh between 14 and 45 kg (31 and 99 lb), making them the heaviest members of the weasel family, but among the smallest marine mammals. Sea otters, whose numbers were once estimated at 150,000-300,000, were hunted extensively for their fur between 1741 and 1911, and the world population fell to 1,000-2,000 individuals living in a fraction of their historic range. A subsequent international ban on hunting, conservation efforts, and reintroduction programs into previously populated areas have contributed to numbers rebounding, and the species now occupies about two-thirds of its former range. The recovery of the sea otter is considered an important success in marine conservation, although populations in the Aleutian Islands and California have recently declined or have plateaued at depressed levels.
Endangered Species Act	The Endangered Species Act of 1973 (Endangered Species Act; 7 U.S.C. § 136, 16 U.S.C. § 1531 et seq). is one of the dozens of United States environmental laws passed in the 1970s. Signed into law by President Richard Nixon on December 28, 1973, it was designed to protect critically imperiled species from extinction as a 'consequence of economic growth and development untempered by adequate concern and conservation.'

Visit Cram101.com for full Practice Exams

18. Conservation of Biodiversity

CHAPTER HIGHLIGHTS & NOTES: KEY TERMS, PEOPLE, PLACES, CONCEPTS

Ecosystem	An ecosystem is a community of living organisms (plants, animals and microbes) in conjunction with the nonliving components of their environment (things like air, water and mineral soil), interacting as a system. These components are regarded as linked together through nutrient cycles and energy flows. As ecosystems are defined by the network of interactions among organisms, and between organisms and their environment, they can come in any size but usually encompass specific, limited spaces (although some scientists say that the entire planet is an ecosystem).
Island biogeography	Island biogeography is a field within biogeography that attempts to establish and explain the factors that affect the species richness of natural communities. The theory was developed to explain species richness of actual islands. It has since been extended to mountains surrounded by deserts, lakes surrounded by dry land, fragmented forest and even natural habitats surrounded by human-altered landscapes.
Biosphere reserves	The Man and the Biosphere Programme (MAB) of UNESCO was established in 1971 to promote interdisciplinary approaches to management, research and education in ecosystem conservation and sustainable use of natural resources. The MAB programme's primary achievement is the creation in 1977 of the World Network of Biosphere Reserves. This World Network is more than a listing -- biosphere reserves exchange knowledge and experiences on sustainable development innovations across national and continental borders -- they exist in more than 100 countries all across the world.
Habitat corridor	A habitat corridor is a strip of land that aids in the movement of species between disconnected areas of their natural habitat. An animal's natural habitat would typically include a number of areas necessary to thrive, such as wetlands, burrowing sites, food, and breeding grounds. Urbanization can split up such areas, causing animals to lose both their natural habitat and the ability to move between regions to use all of the resources they need to survive.
Debt-for-nature swap	Debt-for-nature swaps are financial transactions in which a portion of a developing nation's foreign debt is forgiven in exchange for local investments in environmental conservation measures. The concept of debt-for-nature swaps was first conceived by Thomas Lovejoy of the World Wildlife Fund in 1984 as an opportunity to deal with the problems of developing-nation indebtedness and its consequent deleterious effect on the environment. In the wake of the Latin American debt crisis that resulted in steep reductions to the environmental conservation ability of highly indebted nations, Lovejoy suggested that ameliorating debt and promoting conservation could be done at the same time.

Visit Cram101.com for full Practice Exams

18. Conservation of Biodiversity

CHAPTER QUIZ: KEY TERMS, PEOPLE, PLACES, CONCEPTS

1. A _____ is a biogeographic region with a significant reservoir of biodiversity that is under threat from humans.

   The concept of _____s was originated by Norman Myers in two articles in 'The Environmentalist' (1988), & 1990 revised after thorough analysis by Myers and others in 'Hotspots: Earth's Biologically Richest and Most Endangered Terrestrial Ecoregions'.

   To qualify as a _____ on Myers 2000 edition of the hotspot-map, a region must meet two strict criteria: it must contain at least 0.5% or 1,500 species of vascular plants as endemics, and it has to have lost at least 70% of its primary vegetation.

   a. Biodiversity hotspot
   b. Blue-listed
   c. Buffer zone
   d. Captive breeding

2. In biology and ecology, _____ is the end of an organism or of a group of organisms (taxon), normally a species. The moment of _____ is generally considered to be the death of the last individual of the species, although the capacity to breed and recover may have been lost before this point. Because a species' potential range may be very large, determining this moment is difficult, and is usually done retrospectively.

   a. IUCN Red List
   b. Extinction
   c. PoSAT-1
   d. PROBA

3. The Global Geospace Science (GGS) _____ Satellite was a NASA science spacecraft designed to study the _____ magnetosphere and aurora. It was launched into orbit in February 1996, and continued operations until the program was terminated in April 2008. The spacecraft remains in orbit, though it is now inactive. _____ is the sister ship to GGS Wind.

   a. POLDER
   b. Polar
   c. PoSAT-1
   d. PROBA

4. . _____, FRS (12 February 1809 - 19 April 1882) was an English naturalist. He established that all species of life have descended over time from common ancestors, and proposed the scientific theory that this branching pattern of evolution resulted from a process that he called natural selection, in which the struggle for existence has a similar effect to the artificial selection involved in selective breeding.

   _____ published his theory of evolution with compelling evidence in his 1859 book On the Origin of Species, overcoming scientific rejection of earlier concepts of transmutation of species.

   a. Alfonso Jordan
   b. Polymer Battery Experiment

Visit Cram101.com for full Practice Exams

18. Conservation of Biodiversity

CHAPTER QUIZ: KEY TERMS, PEOPLE, PLACES, CONCEPTS

c. Charles Darwin

d. PROBA

5. The Man and the Biosphere Programme (MAB) of UNESCO was established in 1971 to promote interdisciplinary approaches to management, research and education in ecosystem conservation and sustainable use of natural resources.

The MAB programme's primary achievement is the creation in 1977 of the World Network of _____. This World Network is more than a listing -- _____ exchange knowledge and experiences on sustainable development innovations across national and continental borders -- they exist in more than 100 countries all across the world.

a. Juglone

b. Environmental impact of paint

c. Ethics of terraforming

d. Biosphere reserves

Visit Cram101.com for full Practice Exams

Visit Cram101.com for full Practice Exams

ANSWER KEY
18. Conservation of Biodiversity

1. a
2. b
3. b
4. c
5. d

You can take the complete Chapter Practice Test

for 18. Conservation of Biodiversity
on all key terms, persons, places, and concepts.

Online 99 Cents

http://www.epub89.16.23086.18.cram101.com/

Use www.Cram101.com for all your study needs

including Cram101's online interactive problem solving labs in

chemistry, statistics, mathematics, and more.

Visit Cram101.com for full Practice Exams

19. Global Change

CHAPTER OUTLINE: KEY TERMS, PEOPLE, PLACES, CONCEPTS

Polar

Bioaccumulation

Global change

Global warming

Greenhouse effect

Greenhouse gas

Mount Pinatubo

Denitrification

Montreal Protocol

Intergovernmental Panel on Climate Change

Charles David Keeling

Ice core

Climate model

Thermohaline circulation

Kyoto Protocol

Carbon sequestration

Visit Cram101.com for full Practice Exams

19. Global Change

CHAPTER HIGHLIGHTS & NOTES: KEY TERMS, PEOPLE, PLACES, CONCEPTS

Polar

The Global Geospace Science (GGS) Polar Satellite was a NASA science spacecraft designed to study the polar magnetosphere and aurora. It was launched into orbit in February 1996, and continued operations until the program was terminated in April 2008. The spacecraft remains in orbit, though it is now inactive. Polar is the sister ship to GGS Wind.

Bioaccumulation

Bioaccumulation refers to the accumulation of substances, such as pesticides, or other organic chemicals in an organism. Bioaccumulation occurs when an organism absorbs a toxic substance at a rate greater than that at which the substance is lost. Thus, the longer the biological half-life of the substance the greater the risk of chronic poisoning, even if environmental levels of the toxin are not very high.

Global change

Global change refers to planetary-scale changes in the Earth system. The system consists of the land, oceans, atmosphere, poles, life, the planet's natural cycles and deep Earth processes. These constituent parts influence one another.

Global warming

Global warming refers to the rising average temperature of Earth's atmosphere and oceans, which began to increase in the late 19th century and is projected to continue rising. Since the early 20th century, Earth's average surface temperature has increased by about 0.8 °C (1.4 °F), with about two thirds of the increase occurring since 1980. Warming of the climate system is unequivocal, and scientists are more than 90% certain that most of it is caused by increasing concentrations of greenhouse gases produced by human activities such as deforestation and the burning of fossil fuels. These findings are recognized by the national science academies of all major industrialized nations.[A]

Climate model projections are summarized in the 2007 Fourth Assessment Report (AR4) by the Intergovernmental Panel on Climate Change (IPCC).

Greenhouse effect

The greenhouse effect is a process by which thermal radiation from a planetary surface is absorbed by atmospheric greenhouse gases, and is re-radiated in all directions. Since part of this re-radiation is back towards the surface, energy is transferred to the surface and the lower atmosphere. As a result, the avera surface temperature is higher than it would be if direct heating by solar radiation were the only warming mechanism.

Greenhouse gas

A greenhouse gas is a gas in an atmosphere that absorbs and emits radiation within the thermal infrared range. This process is the fundamental cause of the greenhouse effect. The primary greenhouse gases in the Earth's atmosphere are water vapor, carbon dioxide, methane, nitrous oxide, and ozone.

Mount Pinatubo

Mount Pinatubo is an active stratovolcano located on the island of Luzon, at the intersection of the borders of the Philippine provinces of Zambales, Tarlac, and Pampanga. It is located in the Tri-Cabusilan Mountain range separating the west coast of Luzon from the central plains, and is 42 km (26 mi) west of the dormant and more prominent Mount Arayat, occasionally mistaken for Pinatubo.

Visit Cram101.com for full Practice Exams

19. Global Change

CHAPTER HIGHLIGHTS & NOTES: KEY TERMS, PEOPLE, PLACES, CONCEPTS

Denitrification	Denitrification is a microbially facilitated process of nitrate reduction that may ultimately produce molecular nitrogen (N_2) through a series of intermediate gaseous nitrogen oxide products. This respiratory process reduces oxidized forms of nitrogen in response to the oxidation of an electron donor such as organic matter. The preferred nitrogen electron acceptors in order of most to least thermodynamically favorable include nitrate (NO_3^-), nitrite (NO_2^-), nitric oxide (NO), and nitrous oxide (N_2O).
Montreal Protocol	The Montreal Protocol on Substances That Deplete the Ozone Layer (a protocol to the Vienna Convention for the Protection of the Ozone Layer) is an international treaty designed to protect the ozone layer by phasing out the production of numerous substances believed to be responsible for ozone depletion. The treaty was opened for signature on September 16, 1987, and entered into force on January 1, 1989, followed by a first meeting in Helsinki, May 1989. Since then, it has undergone seven revisions, in 1990 (London), 1991 (Nairobi), 1992 (Copenhagen), 1993 (Bangkok), 1995 (Vienna), 1997 (Montreal), and 1999 (Beijing). It is believed that if the international agreement is adhered to, the ozone layer is expected to recover by 2050. Due to its widespread adoption and implementation it has been hailed as an example of exceptional international co-operation, with Kofi Annan quoted as saying that 'perhaps the single most successful international agreement to date has been the Montreal Protocol'.
Intergovernmental Panel on Climate Change	The Intergovernmental Panel on Climate Change is a scientific intergovernmental body, set up at the request of member governments. It was first established in 1988 by two United Nations organizations, the World Meteorological Organization (WMO) and the United Nations Environment Programme (UNEP), and later endorsed by the United Nations General Assembly through Resolution 43/53. Its mission is to provide comprehensive scientific assessments of current scientific, technical and socio-economic information worldwide about the risk of climate change caused by human activity, its potential environmental and socio-economic consequences, and possible options for adapting to these consequences or mitigating the effects. It is chaired by Rajendra K. Pachauri.
Charles David Keeling	Charles David Keeling was an American scientist whose recording of carbon dioxide at the Mauna Loa Observatory first alerted the world to the possibility of anthropogenic contribution to the 'greenhouse effect' and global warming. The Keeling Curve measures the progressive buildup of carbon dioxide, a greenhouse gas, in the atmosphere.
Ice core	An ice core is a core sample that is typically removed from an ice sheet, most commonly from the polar ice caps of Antarctica, Greenland or from high mountain glaciers elsewhere. As the ice forms from the incremental build up of annual layers of snow, lower layers are older than upper, and an ice core contains ice formed over a range of years. The properties of the ice and the recrystallized inclusions within the ice can then be used to reconstruct a climatic record over the age range of the core, normally through isotopic analysis.

Visit Cram101.com for full Practice Exams

19. Global Change

CHAPTER HIGHLIGHTS & NOTES: KEY TERMS, PEOPLE, PLACES, CONCEPTS

Climate model	Climate models use quantitative methods to simulate the interactions of the atmosphere, oceans, land surface, and ice. They are used for a variety of purposes from study of the dynamics of the climate system to projections of future climate. The most talked-about use of climate models in recent years has been to project temperature changes resulting from increases in atmospheric concentrations of greenhouse gases.
Thermohaline circulation	The term thermohaline circulation refers to the part of the large-scale ocean circulation that is driven by global density gradients created by surface heat and freshwater fluxes. Wind-driven surface currents (such as the Gulf Stream) head polewards from the equatorial Atlantic Ocean, cooling all the while and eventually sinking at high latitudes (forming North Atlantic Deep Water). This dense water then flows into the ocean basins.
Kyoto Protocol	The Kyoto Protocol is a protocol to the United Nations Framework Convention on Climate Change (UNFCCC or FCCC), aimed at fighting global warming. The UNFCCC is an international environmental treaty with the goal of achieving the 'stabilisation of greenhouse gas concentrations in the atmosphere at a level that would prevent dangerous anthropogenic interference with the climate system.' The Protocol was initially adopted on 11 December 1997 in Kyoto, Japan, and entered into force on 16 February 2005. As of September 2011, 191 states have signed and ratified the protocol. The only remaining signatory not to have ratified the protocol is the United States.
Carbon sequestration	Carbon sequestration is the capture of carbon dioxide (CO_2) and may refer specifically to:•'The process of removing carbon from the atmosphere and depositing it in a reservoir.' When carried out deliberately, this may also be referred to as carbon dioxide removal, which is a form of geoengineering.•The process of carbon capture and storage, where carbon dioxide is removed from flue gases, such as on power stations, before being stored in underground reservoirs.•Natural biogeochemical cycling of carbon between the atmosphere and reservoirs, such as by chemical weathering of rocks. Carbon sequestration describes long-term storage of carbon dioxide or other forms of carbon to either mitigate or defer global warming. It has been proposed as a way to slow the atmospheric and marine accumulation of greenhouse gases, which are released by burning fossil fuels. Carbon dioxide is naturally captured from the atmosphere through biological, chemical or physical processes.

Visit Cram101.com for full Practice Exams

19. Global Change

CHAPTER QUIZ: KEY TERMS, PEOPLE, PLACES, CONCEPTS

1. _____ is an active stratovolcano located on the island of Luzon, at the intersection of the borders of the Philippine provinces of Zambales, Tarlac, and Pampanga. It is located in the Tri-Cabusilan Mountain range separating the west coast of Luzon from the central plains, and is 42 km (26 mi) west of the dormant and more prominent Mount Arayat, occasionally mistaken for Pinatubo. Ancestral Pinatubo was a stratovolcano made of andesite and dacite.

   a. Mount Pinatubo
   b. Runaway climate change
   c. Runaway greenhouse effect
   d. Homogenization

2. _____s use quantitative methods to simulate the interactions of the atmosphere, oceans, land surface, and ice. They are used for a variety of purposes from study of the dynamics of the climate system to projections of future climate. The most talked-about use of _____s in recent years has been to project temperature changes resulting from increases in atmospheric concentrations of greenhouse gases.

   a. Climate Science Rapid Response Team
   b. Climate sensitivity
   c. Climate model
   d. GFDL CM2.X

3. _____ is the capture of carbon dioxide (CO_2) and may refer specifically to:•'The process of removing carbon from the atmosphere and depositing it in a reservoir.' When carried out deliberately, this may also be referred to as carbon dioxide removal, which is a form of geoengineering.•The process of carbon capture and storage, where carbon dioxide is removed from flue gases, such as on power stations, before being stored in underground reservoirs.•Natural biogeochemical cycling of carbon between the atmosphere and reservoirs, such as by chemical weathering of rocks.

   _____ describes long-term storage of carbon dioxide or other forms of carbon to either mitigate or defer global warming. It has been proposed as a way to slow the atmospheric and marine accumulation of greenhouse gases, which are released by burning fossil fuels.

   Carbon dioxide is naturally captured from the atmosphere through biological, chemical or physical processes.

   a. reforestation
   b. Juglone
   c. Gibbons v. Ogden
   d. Carbon sequestration

4. . The Global Geospace Science (GGS) _____ Satellite was a NASA science spacecraft designed to study the _____ magnetosphere and aurora. It was launched into orbit in February 1996, and continued operations until the program was terminated in April 2008. The spacecraft remains in orbit, though it is now inactive. _____ is the sister ship to GGS Wind.

   a. Polar
   b. Polymer Battery Experiment

Visit Cram101.com for full Practice Exams

19. Global Change

CHAPTER QUIZ: KEY TERMS, PEOPLE, PLACES, CONCEPTS

c. PoSAT-1

d. PROBA

5. _____ refers to the rising average temperature of Earth's atmosphere and oceans, which began to increase in the late 19th century and is projected to continue rising. Since the early 20th century, Earth's average surface temperature has increased by about 0.8 °C (1.4 °F), with about two thirds of the increase occurring since 1980. Warming of the climate system is unequivocal, and scientists are more than 90% certain that most of it is caused by increasing concentrations of greenhouse gases produced by human activities such as deforestation and the burning of fossil fuels. These findings are recognized by the national science academies of all major industrialized nations.[A]

Climate model projections are summarized in the 2007 Fourth Assessment Report (AR4) by the Intergovernmental Panel on Climate Change (IPCC).

a. Carbon budget

b. Global warming

c. Carbon dioxide flooding

d. Carbon lock-in

Visit Cram101.com for full Practice Exams

Visit Cram101.com for full Practice Exams

ANSWER KEY
19. Global Change

1. a
2. c
3. d
4. a
5. b

You can take the complete Chapter Practice Test

for 19. Global Change
on all key terms, persons, places, and concepts.

Online 99 Cents

http://www.epub89.16.23086.19.cram101.com/

Use www.Cram101.com for all your study needs

including Cram101's online interactive problem solving labs in

chemistry, statistics, mathematics, and more.

Visit Cram101.com for full Practice Exams

20. Sustainability, Economics, and Equity

CHAPTER OUTLINE: KEY TERMS, PEOPLE, PLACES, CONCEPTS

	Kuznets curve
	Ecological economics
	Environmental economics
	Millennium Ecosystem Assessment
	Natural capital
	United Nations Environment Programme
	World Health Organization
	Triple bottom line
	Green Belt Movement
	Environmental justice

CHAPTER HIGHLIGHTS & NOTES: KEY TERMS, PEOPLE, PLACES, CONCEPTS

Kuznets curve	A Kuznets curve is the graphical representation of Simon Kuznets' hypothesis that as a country develops, there is a natural cycle of economic inequality driven by market forces which at first increases inequality, and then decreases it after a certain average income is attained.
	An example of why this happens is that early in development investment opportunities for those who have money multiply, while wages are held down by an influx of cheap rural labor to the cities. Whereas in mature economies, human capital accrual, or an estimate of cost that has been incurred but not yet paid, takes the place of physical capital accrual as the main source of growth; and inequality slows growth by lowering education levels because poor people lack finance for their education in imperfect credit markets.
Ecological economics	Ecological economics is referred to as both a transdisciplinary and interdisciplinary field of academic research that aims to address the interdependence and coevolution of human economies and natural ecosystems over time and space.

Visit Cram101.com for full Practice Exams

20. Sustainability, Economics, and Equity

CHAPTER HIGHLIGHTS & NOTES: KEY TERMS, PEOPLE, PLACES, CONCEPTS

It is distinguished from environmental economics, which is the mainstream economic analysis of the environment, by its treatment of the economy as a subsystem of the ecosystem and its emphasis upon preserving natural capital. One survey of German economists found that ecological and environmental economics are different schools of economic thought, with ecological economists emphasizing 'strong' sustainability and rejecting the proposition that natural capital can be substituted by human-made capital.

Environmental economics	Environmental economics is a subfield of economics concerned with environmental issues. Quoting from the National Bureau of Economic Research Environmental Economics program: Environmental economics is distinguished from Ecological economics that emphasizes the economy as a subsystem of the ecosystem with its focus upon preserving natural capital. One survey of German economists found that ecological and environmental economics are different schools of economic thought, with ecological economists emphasizing 'strong' sustainability and rejecting the proposition that natural capital can be substituted by human-made capital.
Millennium Ecosystem Assessment	The Millennium Ecosystem Assessment, released in 2005, is an international synthesis by over 1000 of the world's leading biological scientists that analyzes the state of the Earth's ecosystems and provides summaries and guidelines for decision-makers. It concludes that human activity is having a significant and escalating impact on the biodiversity of world ecosystems, reducing both their resilience and biocapacity. The report refers to natural systems as humanity's 'life-support system', providing essential 'ecosystem services'.
Natural capital	'Natural capital is the extension of the economic notion of capital (manufactured means of production) to goods and services relating to the natural environment. Natural capital is thus the stock of natural ecosystems that yields a flow of valuable ecosystem goods or services into the future. For example, a stock of trees or fish provides a flow of new trees or fish, a flow which can be indefinitely sustainable.
United Nations Environment Programme	The United Nations Environment Programme coordinates United Nations environmental activities, assisting developing countries in implementing environmentally sound policies and practices. It was founded as a result of the United Nations Conference on the Human Environment in June 1972 and has its headquarters in the Gigiri neighborhood of Nairobi, Kenya. United Nations Environment Programme also has six regional offices and various country offices.
World Health Organization	The World Health Organization is a specialized agency of the United Nations (UN) that is concerned with international public health. It was established on 7 April 1948, with headquarters in Geneva, Switzerland, and is a member of the United Nations Development Group. Its predecessor, the Health Organization, was an agency of the League of Nations.
Triple bottom line	The triple bottom line captures an expanded spectrum of values and criteria for measuring organizational (and societal) success: economic, ecological, and social.

Visit Cram101.com for full Practice Exams

20. Sustainability, Economics, and Equity

CHAPTER HIGHLIGHTS & NOTES: KEY TERMS, PEOPLE, PLACES, CONCEPTS

	With the ratification of the United Nations and ICLEI standard for urban and community accounting in early 2007, this became the dominant approach to public sector full cost accounting. Similar UN standards apply to natural capital and human capital measurement to assist in measurements required by , e.g. the ecoBudget standard for reporting ecological footprint.
Green Belt Movement	The Green Belt Movement is an indigenous grassroots non-governmental organization based in Nairobi, Kenya that takes a holistic approach to development by focusing on environmental conservation, community development and capacity building. Professor Wangari Maathai established the organization in 1977, under the auspices of the National Council of Women of Kenya. The Green Belt Movement organizes women in rural Kenya to plant trees, combat deforestation, restore their main source of fuel for cooking, generate income, and stop soil erosion.
Environmental justice	The term environmental justice emerged as a concept in the United States in the early 1980s. The term has two distinct uses. The first and more common usage describes a social movement in the United States whose focus is on the fair distribution of environmental benefits and burdens.

CHAPTER QUIZ: KEY TERMS, PEOPLE, PLACES, CONCEPTS

1. '_____ is the extension of the economic notion of capital (manufactured means of production) to goods and services relating to the natural environment. _____ is thus the stock of natural ecosystems that yields a flow of valuable ecosystem goods or services into the future. For example, a stock of trees or fish provides a flow of new trees or fish, a flow which can be indefinitely sustainable.

   a. Paleocene-Eocene Thermal Maximum
   b. Paleoclimate Modelling Intercomparison Project
   c. Retreat of glaciers since 1850
   d. Natural capital

2. . _____ is referred to as both a transdisciplinary and interdisciplinary field of academic research that aims to address the interdependence and coevolution of human economies and natural ecosystems over time and space. It is distinguished from environmental economics, which is the mainstream economic analysis of the environment, by its treatment of the economy as a subsystem of the ecosystem and its emphasis upon preserving natural capital. One survey of German economists found that ecological and environmental economics are different schools of economic thought, with ecological economists emphasizing 'strong' sustainability and rejecting the proposition that natural capital can be substituted by human-made capital.

   a. Juglone

Visit Cram101.com for full Practice Exams

20. Sustainability, Economics, and Equity

CHAPTER QUIZ: KEY TERMS, PEOPLE, PLACES, CONCEPTS

b. Ecological economics

c. Mitigation banking

d. Mitigation of peak oil

3. The _____ coordinates United Nations environmental activities, assisting developing countries in implementing environmentally sound policies and practices. It was founded as a result of the United Nations Conference on the Human Environment in June 1972 and has its headquarters in the Gigiri neighborhood of Nairobi, Kenya. _____ also has six regional offices and various country offices.

a. United Nations Environment Programme

b. Odyssey

c. Endangered Species Act

d. Roman Warm Period

4. The _____ captures an expanded spectrum of values and criteria for measuring organizational (and societal) success: economic, ecological, and social. With the ratification of the United Nations and ICLEI standard for urban and community accounting in early 2007, this became the dominant approach to public sector full cost accounting. Similar UN standards apply to natural capital and human capital measurement to assist in measurements required by , e.g. the ecoBudget standard for reporting ecological footprint.

a. Value of Earth

b. Triple bottom line

c. Wood-free paper

d. Xeriscaping

5. A _____ is the graphical representation of Simon Kuznets' hypothesis that as a country develops, there is a natural cycle of economic inequality driven by market forces which at first increases inequality, and then decreases it after a certain average income is attained.

An example of why this happens is that early in development investment opportunities for those who have money multiply, while wages are held down by an influx of cheap rural labor to the cities. Whereas in mature economies, human capital accrual, or an estimate of cost that has been incurred but not yet paid, takes the place of physical capital accrual as the main source of growth; and inequality slows growth by lowering education levels because poor people lack finance for their education in imperfect credit markets.

a. Land economy

b. Manfred Max Neef

c. Mitigation banking

d. Kuznets curve

Visit Cram101.com for full Practice Exams

Visit Cram101.com for full Practice Exams

ANSWER KEY
20. Sustainability, Economics, and Equity

1. d
2. b
3. a
4. b
5. d

You can take the complete Chapter Practice Test

for 20. Sustainability, Economics, and Equity
on all key terms, persons, places, and concepts.

Online 99 Cents

http://www.epub89.16.23086.20.cram101.com/

Use www.Cram101.com for all your study needs

including Cram101's online interactive problem solving labs in

chemistry, statistics, mathematics, and more.

Visit Cram101.com for full Practice Exams

Other Cram101 e-Books and Tests

Want More? Cram101.com...

Cram101.com provides the outlines and highlights of your textbooks, just like this e-StudyGuide, but also gives you the PRACTICE TESTS, and other exclusive study tools for all of your textbooks.

Learn More. *Just click*
http://www.cram101.com/

Other Cram101 e-Books and Tests

Visit Cram101.com for full Practice Exams

CPSIA information can be obtained at www.ICGtesting.com
Printed in the USA
LVOW11s2216170714

394799LV00002B/52/P